How  Smile

14 Ways to a Better You

ROBERT M. COLE , MD

Published by RMC Publishing Company

Copyright © 2020 Robert M. Cole IV, MD

All rights reserved.

ISBN: 9798690242718

www.robertmcolemd.com

DEDICATION

This book is dedicated to my family, who remain the epicenter of my life. To my parents, who raised me and instilled in me the foundation of positivity and hard work. Despite my sometimes-erratic behavior as an adolescent and young adult, you never wavered in your constant guidance and support. To my wife Sara and son Luke, you are the best part of every day, and you always make me smile the most. Thank you to the many other family members who have molded me into the man I was able to become, and specifically my siblings: Chris, Stephen and Melanie.

DISCLAIMER

The ideas and concepts in this book are my opinion. In no way is this book written to help treat clinical depression or anxiety. If you are concerned about depression or anxiety, it is imperative to contact a physician in order to best receive the proper treatment.

Table of Contents

Introduction **15**

Chapter 1: Through a Toddler's Eyes **23**

    The Power of Perception 28

    The Story of Two Dogs 31

    How Can We Change Our Ways? 32

Chapter 2: Feed the Right Wolf **39**

    Don't Be a Victim 40

    The Problem with Self-Pity 43

    Put an End to Self-Pity 47

Chapter 3: Do Not Fear Failure **55**

    Eliminate Your Fear 57

    My Experience with Failure 61

    Learn to Embrace Failure 66

Chapter 4: See the Forest **71**

    Ants and Elephants 72

    The Man and the Construction Workers 76

    Do Not Let Details Paralyze Your Plan of Action 78

    The 80 / 20 Rule 80

How to Better See the Forest 83

Chapter 5: Find Your Light (In and at the End of the Tunnel) 87

The Power of Pleasure 88

A Bit More about Future Mental Time Travel 91

How to Light Your Tunnel 96

Chapter 6: Don't Take it Personally 99

What Is Your Emotional Type? 101

Why Are We So Sensitive? 104

How Sensitive Are You? 108

Chapter 7: Forgive and Move On 115

Imperfection and Mortality 117

Eliminate Grudges 120

Forgive Yourself and Eliminate Guilt 122

The Power of Forgiveness 126

Chapter 8: Find Your Purpose, Pursue Your Passion 129

Job, Career, and Passion 131

Passion, Hobby, and Dreams 134

Finding My Passion 136

Chapter 9: Disconnect 143

Addicted and Depressed 145

My Departure from the Social Media World 153

Take the Challenge 156

Chapter 10: Be Present in the Moment 159

The Magic Thread 159

Live in the Now 164

Stop Worrying and Start Acting 168

The Importance of Reducing Anxiety 170

Seven Ways to Be More Present and Reduce Anxiety 172

Chapter 11: Be Patient, but Do Not Wait Around 175

A World of Instant Gratification 177

Learning to Sacrifice 179

Don't Wait Around 182

Chapter 12: Laugh Often. Sometimes at Yourself. Sometimes at Your Life 187

The Three Things We Should Do Every Day ... 187

Learning to Laugh 190

Chapter 13: Move 199

Chapter 14: Kill Them with Kindness 205

Getting Ahead by Getting Along 208

When Being Kind Is Tough 210

References 217

Introduction

"Just have fun," she said in a soft and raspy voice. "I always had fun, and it's been a good life. And dance. I wish I could go back to those days when I was young and dance again." She lay there, too weak to lift her head off the bed, and she smiled. She went on, "There is a lot bad in this world if you let it get to you. But you just have to smile and keep moving. Then you will realize it is not as bad as people make it out to be."

It was her last day on Earth, and at 92 years old she had lived a full life. Her family surrounded her, and with fear and pain in their eyes they said goodbye to their beloved grandmother and mother. In her last hours she remained the rock her family saw her as, and she gracefully left this world.

Encounters such as this in the intensive care unit (ICU) are plentiful, and over the years I have witnessed many. They have taught me the power of words and the amazing strength of humanity. People like the dying woman above have reaffirmed for me the simplicity of what brings joy in life. It is not about what you have or where you have been. It is about how you feel and the strength of your attitude in every moment. How will you make other people feel? What will you have to say in your final hours when you look back at your life? How will *you* feel?

In time, I have realized that it is OK. It is OK for me to fail and feel embarrassed. It is OK that life is not always fair and that other people may not like me. I realized I am incredibly imperfect. I can finally appreciate that it is not about what may come, or the mistakes I made in the past. It is not about what could have been or the uncertainty of the future. It is about what is happening right now. How can I make *now* better for myself and the people around me? How can I be the best version of myself in this moment? I knew little about the woman in the above story. I only knew the strength she showed in that moment. I only knew the pain felt by the loved ones she left behind.

Through time, I have learned that changing the way I perceive life events can in turn change the very world I live in. I had an awakening about the fragility and finite nature of life and the pure absurdity of complaining and dwelling in negativity or anger. It takes energy to be upset, but being content and happy fuels your soul and mind. I learned that it takes a combination of action and patience to conquer this ever-changing and harsh world . . . and then it will not seem so harsh. I learned these things through the passing of time, my observation of others, my own failures, through education, and by surrounding myself with the right people.

Since discovering these new tactics, I have found it more difficult to sit on the sidelines when others are unhappy. Watching a loved one or one of my colleagues tussle with life's many challenges has always bothered me. I have always been tempted to pick people up when I see them in a state of need. Over time, I've come to the realization that on most occasions I have been extremely ineffective in helping. There are probably multiple reasons for this, but mostly that my jumbled mind is unsuccessful in verbalizing the important points that can make a difference. Writing has always been my preferred way to communicate, and in many ways this book is based on years of things I meant to say or tried to say, but was not quite eloquent enough to convey. It is a combination of those tactics which I have learned and practice daily, and others which I am still mastering.

I grew up in a home where negativity and self-pity were not accepted, and I was heavily influenced by my father's inspirational nightly talks and never-ending words of advice. Even for me, his positivity can still be nauseating at times. But it was influential. He would often quote a slew of South Jersey and New England natives with funny nicknames who had a knack for simplifying the tribulations of life. Despite this upbringing, I often struggled to uphold these valuable teachings in the real world, and I settled for a lesser version of myself on so many occasions in life. I have come to realize that obtaining happiness and being positive is not just something you wake up and do every day because you want to; life is much more complicated than that. It takes time to master this, and the result is imperfect in nature. But only you can control the outcome of your life and the emotional state of being you choose to navigate with.

Failures and challenges during my pursuit of medicine, capped off recently by the COVID-19 pandemic, inspired me to finally put to paper the tactics I have used the last 15 years to deal with adversity, stay positive, take control of my life, and keep smiling. This book is what I tried to say to so many people on so many occasions. Even as I wrote this book, I had to remind myself of the tactics I have learned through the years. I am a work in progress.

This book is not me telling anyone how to live their life and is not meant to judge others. I am not worthy of judging anyone. It is not meant to cure depression or anxiety and fix all your problems. No one smiles all the time. Happiness and smiles hold value because they contrast with the times of frowns and unhappiness; they are all variations of the natural changes in mood we all have. Without a little rain, a sunny day will lose its luster.

This is a healthy mix of stories, parables, quotes, and evidence, constructed into advice based on my own experience and those of the people who have influenced me thus far in my life. If this book helps even one reader solve one problem in their life, or makes one person smile, I deem it a success.

Chapter 1: Through a Toddler's Eyes

"Your perspective will either become your prison or your passport."

–Steven Furtick

In 1997, the movie *Life is Beautiful* was released. The film takes place in the darkest of human times, when the Nazi regime had a grip on most of Europe, entrenched in fear, racism, violence, and destruction. In this movie, the main character, Guido, goes to extraordinary and creative lengths to convince his toddler son Giosué that life under German rule is actually a complex game. He would get points for listening to his father and completing certain tasks, and lose points if he cried, complained he was hungry, or missed his mother. Guido created an alternative universe for his child to help shield him from the horrors of death, anguish, and pain. Guido knew that if he could help alter his son's perception of reality, he could save him from a lifetime of pain. He could turn fear into fun, his anxiety into adrenaline. In the worst of times, he could give his son hope. He recognized the power of altering perception.

Can we live in an alternative world which is shielded from reality, like a toddler influenced by his father? No. But we can learn a lot from this movie. We can learn that there is power in perception and perspective. How we perceive the world determines everything. It is what makes reality a good day or a bad day. It is important to remember that reality is what you perceive it to be. Real life events do not exist in isolation. Instead, they only exist in the form in which they are interpretated by each person. Therefore, each of us independently control reality, even if we do little to affect what is occurring.

How each of us chooses to view certain material things is a good example of differing perspective. For example, a pair of shoes a person sees as beautiful, someone else may see as downright ugly. But are they ugly or are they beautiful? Neither. They are shoes. They keep your feet warm and dry. You were fortunate enough to have the money to buy shoes. Some people have no shoes. In fact, nearly 1 billion people on earth (more than 10% of inhabitants) lack adequate footwear. Regardless of having the proper resources to afford shoes, some people are too sick to go outside and have a need for such material things. The shoes may be an odd color or not fit perfectly, but you are healthy enough to need them and have the means to afford them. Are they still ugly?

Have you ever returned from a tropical vacation back to a colder climate and felt a deep, overwhelming chill when you walked out of the airport? You have a new expectation about how you *think* you should feel, influenced by your new perspective. For someone from Greenland or parts of Alaska, 45-50 degrees may be the nicest day in months, will drive people outside and into parks, and make them feel genuinely comfortable. But that same temperature in a traditionally hotter environment, like Florida, will be a different reality. People will complain it is way too cold. The parks and outside restaurants will be empty.

Same temperature. Same day. Different people. Different perspective. Different outcome. If you could see the weather through the eyes of both regional inhabitants, perhaps there would be very few days when you were not happy with the temperature. Reminding yourself that the weather on a certain day is in fact "not so bad" is just a small example of how altering your perspective can lead to more satisfaction. This practice can be applied to larger and more impactful life events.

Our perspective, which is essentially our attitude or how we regard something, will strongly affect how we perceive things. How we perceive things in life will strongly affect our gratitude, appreciation, happiness, and overall mood. How we perceive the world is therefore a product of who we surround ourselves with, what we chose to prioritize and whether or not we have the capability to sift through the weeds of negativity that try to bring us down. Perception is always changing, differs between individuals, and is often a choice. Changing how you view the world changes the world.

Now that is power.

The Power of Perception

There are well-respected theories indicating that clinically depressed individuals have an altered perception of reality. In a recent study that examined abnormal time experiences in depression, individuals tended to report the domination of the past over the present and future. In addition, depression seemed to produce a subjective slowing of time in study participants.[1]

This is an example of how someone's frame of mind and mood can powerfully affect their perception of reality. People believe that time is moving slower simply based on certain chemical imbalances in their brain (depression). It seems clear that how we interpret everyday events becomes strongly tied to our emotional state.

In addition to our state of mind, surrounding ourselves with positive environment will surely influence how we perceive the world. Let us look at another example. In two experiments published in *The Journal of Psychological Science*, researchers found that participants interpreted a neutral face as smiling more frequently when it was paired with an unseen positive image.

Using a technique called continuous flash suppression, the researchers were able to present stimuli to participants without them knowing it. In one experiment, 43 participants were shown a series of flashing images, which alternated between a pixelated image and a neutral face, presented to their dominant eye. At the same time, a low-contrast image of a smiling, scowling, or neutral face was presented to their non-dominant eye. Typically, this low-contrast image will be suppressed by the stimulus presented to the dominant eye, and participants will not consciously see it.

At the end of each trial, participants were asked to choose which face matched the one they saw during the test from a set of five different faces. Remember that they only consciously saw a face with a neutral expression. Participants who were subconsciously shown a smiling face tended to pick other smiles as the best match.[2]

We see with this simple experiment that what and who we are exposed to in our personal environment, even if we are not aware of it, will influence our perception. Who and what you choose to surround yourself with can change everything. Surround yourself with positive energy, and you will perhaps view the world in the same light.

The Story of Two Dogs

As we strive to surround our self with positive energy, we must also appreciate the magnitude of our personal state of mind. There is a story they tell of two dogs. Both at separate times walk into the same room. One comes out wagging his tail, while the other comes out growling. A woman watching this goes into the room to see what could possibly make one dog so happy and the other so mad. To her surprise she finds a room filled with mirrors. The happy dog found a thousand happy dogs looking back at him, while the angry dog saw only angry dogs growling back at him. What you see in the world is a reflection of who you are. [3]

While surrounding yourself with quality people and creating a positive environment is key to gaining a new perspective in life, there is no more important influence than your own mind. It starts with you, and once you develop the ability to smile more often, appreciate the gifts in life, and express this, you will build the foundation for a new way to look at reality.

How Can We Change Our Ways?

So how can you change your perspective to give you a better appreciation of the world and your potential? This may seem impossible, since how we perceive the world is not only subjective, but also immensely complicated. Neither I nor anyone else can directly change how you view the world. However, through some simple changes, we can *indirectly* influence how we perceive reality. So where do we begin with attempting to alter our perception in a positive manner? Try the following five tactics and you will likely see an improvement in how you view the world.

1. Surround Yourself with Others Who Have a Positive Attitude. The old saying, "Tell me who you walk with and I'll tell you who you are," has always influenced me. There are several ways to interpret this simple saying. Those individuals that you spend time with and are seen with in public will change the perception of who you are in the eyes of others. In addition, I have always interpreted it to emphasize that the people you surround yourself with will influence who you become and play a role in the decisions you make. Positive people will help reinforce the good in life and can be a constant reminder of your full potential. They will help show us how to act and how to better view the world. Like the subconscious images from the previously mentioned study, they have the power to turn a neutral situation into something more positive, even if we are unaware.

2. Avoid Negative People. Impossible, right? On most days you will be forced to interact with people who are inherently negative. They will always attempt to bring you down. They will complain, share rumors about other people's failures, and tempt you to engage in their rhetoric. These negative individuals are trapped in a prison of discontent. They want desperately for you to join them in their jail cell. Their constant barrage of damaging behavior and verbal pandering make them feel entitled and powerful. But they are the very opposite. They are weak, and until they change their ways, they will remain in a state of emotional suffering. Resist and minimize your time with these individuals. Life is too short to dwell in negativity.

3. Avoid or Minimize Negative Media Content. The constant dramatization and relentless reporting of unfortunate events will not only lead to anxiety and fear, but will subconsciously change the natural way you view the world. The studies available on the relationship between news exposure and effect generally support the notion that exposure to news reports changes our mood and state of mind, inherently affecting our perspective. More specifically, several experimental studies found a direct relationship between negative news exposure and negative emotional states. After being exposed to negative news reports, positive emotions decreased, whereas negative emotions, sadness, worry, and anxiety increased. Other studies have found that news exposure can indirectly cause psychological distress and negative affect through an increase in stress levels and irrational beliefs or depression. [4]

4. Be Grateful. By reflecting on what we already have in a positive manner and training our brains to do this regularly, we will maintain a much more positive mood, and this will inherently affect the way we perceive the world. Do this every day at some point. Be thankful for the people that surround you, for your career, and for the simple necessities like food, shelter, and running water. Most people on Earth are not guaranteed these basic things. Be thankful for the simple things in life—it will go a long way. Self-help author Melody Beattie said it best: "Gratitude turns what we have into enough, and more. It turns denial into acceptance, chaos into order, confusion into clarity. It makes sense of our past, brings peace for today, and creates a vision for tomorrow."

5. Challenge Yourself to Learn. Self-help books offer great tools for how to cope with challenging times and improve your outlook on life. The number of titles is endless, and every individual will have their preference. As you expand your mind you will develop the power to control perception more gracefully and effectively.

Building a smile starts with learning to change your perception and perspective.

Chapter 2: Feed the Right Wolf

"Self-pity is our worst enemy, and if we yield to it, we can never do anything wise in this world."

–Helen Keller

There is a Native American parable which has been passed on for generations. It is the story of the two wolves.

An old Cherokee was teaching his grandson about life. "A fight is going on inside me," he said to the boy. "It is a terrible fight between two wolves. One is evil: He is anger, envy, sorrow, regret, greed, arrogance, self-pity, guilt, resentment, inferiority, lies, false pride, superiority, and ego."

He continued, "The other is good: He is joy, peace, love, hope, serenity, humility, kindness, benevolence, empathy, generosity, truth, compassion, and faith. The same fight is going on inside you—and inside every other person, too."

The grandson thought about it for a minute and then asked his grandfather, "Which wolf will win, Grandpa?"

The old Cherokee simply replied, "The one you feed." [5]

Only WE have control of what emotions and feelings we let proliferate in our mind. Which wolf will you chose to feed?

Don't Be a Victim

Helen Keller could not see or hear. Sit and imagine that for a minute. I sometimes get annoyed from a mild headache when reading too much or if my beer gets hot on the beach. I have witnessed adults turn into children and pout when their latte wasn't made correctly. Helen could not see, though she learned to read through touch. She could not hear, yet went on to influence millions, and eventually earn a bachelor's degree from Radcliffe College. She refused to be a victim when she had perhaps every right to play that role. [6]

Oprah Winfrey has become one of the most influential individuals in the world, and has amassed incredible wealth in the process. Oprah also had every reason to be a victim. An African American woman born into poverty, she famously wore potato sacks because they could not afford dresses. She was abused as a child. She became pregnant at age 14 and lost the child. But if Oprah had embraced the tempting role of being a victim, there would have been no award-winning talk show, no OWN Media Network, no Harpo Films or *O Magazine*.[7]

Bad things will happen in life. Challenges and uncertainty are a part of any road forward. You may fail a class, lose a job, deal with a health issue, or struggle in a relationship. How we respond to tragedy and difficult situations is what will set us on the right path in life. One of the most devastating traits, and a common reaction to a difficult time, is the trap of falling into self-pity. The minute you accept your role as a victim, you have committed to being a victim, often for an extended period of time.

Once you think of yourself as a victim you will find excuses to maintain that status. "I have not received a promotion because my boss doesn't like me." "I am overweight because I have poor genetics and no time for exercising." "I can't find a life partner because I am not likable." You can easily find excuses to NOT succeed, NOT make good decisions, NOT take responsibility, and NOT to take a risk. These excuses will become more creative with time as you find different themes to attach to, building walls around yourself, and limiting any chance of escaping your current situation. Self-pity is the easy road, and a road traveled by many people, though rarely a trait of a leader or successful person. It is rarely a trait of genuinely happy individuals.

The Problem with Self-Pity

Self-pity does nothing more than perpetuate depression and self-destructive tendencies, and will prevent you from reaching your potential in life. A study published in *the Journal of Personality* found that with respect to personality, there was a strong association between self-pity and neuroticism, in particular depression. In addition, individuals that scored high in self-pity traits also showed generalized externality beliefs, meaning they saw themselves as governed by circumstances beyond their control. [8]

Life is chaotic, challenging, and oftentimes overwhelming. If you believe that you are the victim—thrown into the abyss with no control—you will let uncontrollable events and other people guide you. You will relinquish control of your life. Instead, change your perception when challenges arise. When things do not go your way, embrace the events as a time to learn and grow. Immediately put the events into perspective and recognize that things could always be worse. Take control of the situation and stay away from excuses.

American novelist John Gardner expressed these sentiments well, saying, "Self-pity is easily the most destructive of the non-pharmaceutical narcotics; it is addictive, gives momentary pleasure and separates the victim from reality." In the book *Tiny Beautiful Things*, Cheryl Strayed described feeling sorry for herself, saying, "Self-pity is a dead-end road. You make the choice to drive down it. It's up to you to decide to stay parked there or to turn around and drive out."

Recently, a friend of mine was venting to me about the challenges of filling out unemployment forms during the COVID pandemic. They described how complex the application was, how access was only available on limited days, and that the money was not ideal. They went on and on. In a matter of minutes, they had let everyone in the room know that they were the victim. The individual was complaining so we could all hear. Rather than expressing gratitude for a home, she complained. Rather than being grateful for financial support, she focused on the frustration it caused. This family member is typically a positive and happy individual, but self-pity is tempting to us all.

On the contrary, I have seen great examples of appreciation and strength during this same period. I have had several COVID-19 patients on life support, some for as long as 21 days. During this time, family members were not permitted to see their loved ones. Imagine your loved one on the verge of death, and you cannot be present to support them. Yet in this difficult time, most families remained extremely thankful for just a daily five-minute phone call. They would thank our team endlessly and never complained. They accepted the circumstances and never fell into the trap of self-pity. They refused to make the tragedy of a pandemic about themselves. I believe this positive attitude is what enables humans to endure, and should be practiced in both the best and worst of times.

Put an End to Self-Pity

Do you find yourself making excuses for being unhappy in your career or in your relationships? Do you spend a portion of your time with others complaining about problems in your life? Do you often feel like life has been unfair to you, and others just don't understand? Do you find yourself sometimes asking *why me?*

You are not alone if you said yes to any of these questions. It is a common defense mechanism for humans to victimize themselves to rationalize failure, feelings of discontent, and unhappiness. Let us look at ways we can help prevent self-pity from proliferating.

1. Stop Complaining to Other People. Whether it's a fender bender that resulted in financial hardship, having to work extra hours to accomplish a task in your career, or the weather that ruined your plans—As we voice our complaints out loud, we continue the slow, convincing process of becoming a victim. Occasional venting is healthy but becoming obsessed with expressing our discontent to others is counterproductive. Some people get enjoyment out of complaining because it gives them a sense of entitlement. It makes them feel powerful; even if just for a second. In reality, we give others the misconception that we are in fact weak, and can appear less likable. Philosopher Eckhart Tolle said, "When you complain, you make yourself a victim. Leave the situation, change the situation, or accept it. All else is madness."

2. Verbalize Your Gratitude. When I work long stretches in the ICU, the nurses sometimes express empathy about my long hours. My response is always the same: "I am lucky to have a job, and I love my job." The more I say those words, the more I convince myself they are true. More importantly, speaking my gratitude out loud helps prevent giving in to becoming a victim. The key is to verbalize your appreciation for what you have in life. Research supports the idea that grateful thinking can improve subjective wellbeing and mood. In the *Journal of Research and Personality,* published in 2008, two longitudinal studies found that gratitude led to higher levels of perceived social support and lower levels of stress and depression. [9] In the words of motivational speaker Zig Ziglar, "Gratitude is the healthiest of all human emotions. The more you express gratitude for what you have, the more likely you will have even more to express gratitude for."

3. Don't Make Excuses, Make Different Choices. Benjamin Franklin eloquently and simply stated, "He that is good at making excuses is seldom good for anything else."

My profession has allowed me the opportunity to meet people who work in many different roles. Often I hear the same employees complaining over and over again about why they do not like their boss or their daily tasks. They go on and on in bitter detail, week after week. Month after month. Year after year. They actively embrace their role as a victim—yet every day they make a choice to stay in that specific job. Every day they could choose a new employer or career, yet they choose to maintain their status as a victim. Rather than making a change, they choose to fester in self-pity in an addicting fashion. "Everything in your life is a reflection of a choice you have made. If you want a different result, make a different choice."[10]

4. Stop Blaming Others When Things Go Wrong; Try Blaming Yourself. When you take responsibility for your own part in events, you do several important things. You reinforce owning your decisions. You show strength in the eyes of others. You allow yourself to internally reflect, adjust, and make improvements. You also set yourself apart as a leader, someone willing to carry the trials and tribulations of others. Blaming others is easy, immature, and often ineffective. Blaming yourself is challenging, mature, and allows for control of a situation, rather than passing that control to someone else. Author Steve Goodier spoke of his decision to stop blaming, saying, "An important decision I made was to resist playing the Blame Game. The day I realized that I am in charge of how I approach problems in my life, that things will turn out better or worse because of me and nobody else, that was the day I knew I would be a happier and healthier person. And that was the day I knew I could truly build a life that matters." Take my and Steve's advice: stop playing the blame game.

5. Stop Asking Why. *Why is this happening to me? Why doesn't he or she like me? Why don't I get paid enough?* When we continually ask these questions, we train our minds to practice self-pity subconsciously. Instead of asking why, we should rephrase these questions in our head: *How can I keep this from happening to me again? What can I do so he or she likes me more? How can I make more money?*

What are the next steps in righting my situation? What can I learn from this unfortunate situation?

Once you have eliminated excuses and the concept of being a victim, you will free yourself from the prison of mediocrity and despair. You will begin to find solutions to your problems rather than searching for another outlet to express your discontent. Solutions lead to progress, accomplishments, and happiness. People will quickly begin to view you as strong-willed and you will develop a natural ability to persevere.

Building a smile starts with the elimination of self-pity.

Chapter 3: Do Not Fear Failure

"I've missed more than 9,000 shots in my career. I've lost almost 300 games. Twenty-six times I've been trusted to take the game-winning shot and missed. I've failed over and over and over again in my life. And that is why I succeed."

–Michael Jordan

Michael Jordan was arguably the greatest basketball player of all time. He turned basketball into an international sport, and he is one of the most recognized athletes of the last 100 years. If he had been too scared to keep taking those game-winning shots after missing a few, he never would have achieved the same degree of success, and Air Jordan would never be the universal brand it is today.

Abraham Lincoln, one of the most well-known historical figures of the last 500 years, knew what it felt like to fail. He lost his job, took part in a failed business venture, and lost multiple political races before he ever made it to the White House. He once famously said, "Success is going from failure to failure without losing enthusiasm." Abraham Lincoln never lost his enthusiasm to succeed. He would go on to liberate millions of African Americans and help save the nation after the Civil War. He is regularly rated by historians as the greatest US president.

Have you ever heard of the business enterprise Traf-O-Data? You probably have not, because it went out of business more than 40 years ago. It was just one of entrepreneur Bill Gates's failures on his road to success. He was also a

Harvard dropout, yet he would go on to form the world's largest software company and become one of the wealthiest men in the world.[11] How about Laugh-o-gram studios? Have you heard of that one? That was Walt Disney's failed business venture. He would also notoriously get fired from a newspaper for not being creative enough. The Walt Disney Company is now one of the largest mass media companies in the world. [12]

Failure is inevitable, even for the most successful people on earth. Failure helps us grow and it gives us each an opportunity to reflect and improve. Without failure, there would be no success.

Eliminate Your Fear

Understanding your personal fear of failure is not only necessary to obtain more success, but also to better establish a positive mood and attitude. I cannot stress enough the emotional importance of conquering, understanding, and harnessing this fear. For example, fear of failure in college students has been shown to be associated with high levels of worry, anxiety, cognitive disruption and low levels of optimism. There seems to be several presumed consequences of failure: experiencing shame and embarrassment, devaluing one's self-esteem, having an uncertain future, and losing the interest of loved ones. [13] In summary, evidence seems to support there is a real emotional burden regarding fearing failure, therefore controlling this fear is of great importance.

Have you ever found excuses to delay something in life because you were so concerned you would let others down? Maybe you did not want to purse a promotion at work, so you found every excuse to not apply for the new position in an effort to avoid the potential failure of not getting it. You delay and delay and wait until you finally gather the courage to make a move. Once you do, you realize you wasted a significant amount of time lamenting in fear.

See, even with tasks that we do end up accomplishing, the fear of failure can many times delay our success. This idea was supported by an article published in *the Advances of Health Sciences Education*, which found that fear of failure was often associated with academic procrastination in undergraduate students. Other studies have demonstrated that the dread of embarrassment causes male undergraduates to procrastinate to avoid the possibility of failure.[14] The fear of failure and its connection to procrastination can be extrapolated from the educational setting as it really applies to all facets of life and across all demographics. It is fair to say that if we fear failure, we will use procrastination as a strong defense mechanism to avoid the task at hand or delay it, often leading to more anxiety and distress.

What I have observed is that people often fear failure to the point that most become paralyzed. The idea of losing something or letting people down often overpowers the thought of success. Failure has the misperception of being negative, embarrassing and abnormal. This idea of failure as negative is what must change in your mind in order for you to better obtain the happy state you desire. We have an opportunity to perhaps reduce anxiety, increase optimism, boost our self-esteem and stop procrastinating.

My Experience with Failure

My wife had had a tough day at work. When I tried to motivate her, she made the mistake of telling me, "Well, it always just works out for you. You don't know what it's like to fail!" I sat there and thought about what she said. Maybe she was right. Maybe I had been blessed with great parents, all the material things necessary for success, and pure luck. Maybe I always just fell into the right situation.

There is no doubt I have been fortunate, and without the support of my family I would likely not have reached my full potential. But when I think back over the last decades, I can say life has been far from perfect. Failure hit me in the face on many occasions, and my fear of failure limited my potential.

My college career, for example, started with complete and utter disappointment. I failed out of chemistry and dropped out of two other classes. In a matter of weeks my parents received a refund from my college, as I was no longer a full-time student. In my dad's famous words, "You better get it together, boy." Well, maybe there were some other choice words thrown in there, too.

I had failed. What was even worse, I stopped putting the time into studying, because I was afraid that if I worked hard and then did poorly on a test, I would look like a fool. Outside the classroom, I did not try out for the track team like I had always dreamed of doing. I feared not making the team, despite having running times that made me competitive. I missed out on countless opportunities because I was afraid of failing.

I would eventually work hard enough to improve my GPA. My father urged me to learn from my failures. He used this opportunity to ingrain in me a mentality of accepting failure as part of the process, and to stay persistent in chasing my dreams. I wanted desperately to erase the disappointment from my parents' faces. I wanted to be a physician. Unfortunately, I had neither the grades, the MCAT score, nor the patience to attend a medical school in the United States. I remember vividly when my college guidance counselor sat me down in his office and broke the news in a calming southern drawl. "You can become a doctor, but you won't be doing it here in the States."

On a whim, I decided to attend a medical school in Mexico where my cousin was a student at the time. My undergraduate college record, from an academic achievement standpoint, was a failure—but just in time, my efforts bought me a ticket to the next round of playoffs in the game of life. Hope was not lost.

Medical school in a foreign country was both terrifying, exciting, and challenging. Shockingly, after about a month in school, I made the decision to abandon my dream, no longer pursue medicine, and head back home. I feared my time would be lost and that my heart was no longer in it. I made every excuse to leave. I was too far from home. I did not understand Spanish. It cost too much money. I was no longer interested.

While there were many factors in my decision, looking back, what drove most of my choice to abort my dream was the fear of failure. I famously called my brother and told him I would be a pursuing a job as an exterminator from an ad I found online. Perfect—it would be hard to fail at my new venture. He still brings this up from time to time and makes fun of me. I stopped going to class and started planning my next move. A career full of killing bugs!

One absence short of being expelled, in the last hour, my wonderful family and friends convinced me to stay the rest of the year. "Just give it a fair chance; it's OK if it doesn't work out," my mom said. It was one of the most important turning points in my life. At that moment I accepted the fact that failure was a real possibility . . . and that was perfectly OK. Understanding this allowed me to enjoy my pursuit of a dream, separate from the fear of being embarrassed if things did not work out as planned.

I would eventually push through medical school, excel on my medical boards, and pursue a career in critical care medicine. There would be many failed tests, failed relationships, poor decisions, and disappointments. I have failed many times since then, but have tried not to let fear deter my pursuit of happiness and success. Failure has molded me into the imperfect human I am, and the acceptance of those failures has made me a happier man.

Learn to Embrace Failure

How has the fear of failure affected the way you approach life? Are you ever afraid to be passionate about a certain idea or new challenge, because if you fail you might be embarrassed? Are the opinions of others driving some of your decision making? Does the idea of failure often make you think twice about pursuing a new venture in life? If failure were not an option, what risks would you take to obtain success? If you knew you could not fail, what would you be doing right now? Do you procrastinate at times to avoid failure?

As you move forward in life, embrace the possibility of failure. Dig deep and push through. Be inspired by those that have repeatedly failed but have gone on to succeed. Tony Robbins gave excellent advice about how to get over your fear of failure: you should learn to fear the idea of *not* taking action and settling for a life that is below what you deserve and desire, rather than failing at *the action itself*. You must train yourself to use the energy of fear to your advantage and accept that when you do decide to pursue something you fear, it may not feel perfect. That is OK. [15]

I have a few additional pieces of advice:

1. Embrace your strengths to improve your self-esteem. This will inherently lead to less fear of failure.

2. Block out the opinions of others as you pursue your dreams. Remember, weak people talk, but strength comes from action. Stay focused on the outcomes that matter and shield yourself from the chatter that doesn't matter.

3. Stop procrastinating. By doing this, you set a standard and expectation that you will not allow hesitation to be a subconscious tool to feed your fear.

4. Accept uncertainty. Sometimes the fear of not knowing what the future brings is far worse than the actual future. This fear, as mentioned, will paralyze people into inaction. Life is short, and excitement and happiness stem from pushing through challenges and conquering our fears.

Whether it is a career, relationship, competitive sport or learning a new hobby. Obtaining success after failing has the potential to bring happiness and the acceptance of this imperfect process will make life much more gratifying.

Building a smile starts with accepting failure.

Chapter 4: See the Forest

"If you spend your life overanalyzing every encounter you will always see the trees, but never the forest."

–Shannon Alder

Any experienced physician will tell you that at some point they had to suffer through a detailed, drawn out, and unorganized presentation by an intern. A simple patient presentation about respiratory failure from asthma becomes a dissertation on the patient's life and medical history. By the end, the intern has lost the attention of the group, and often cannot even understand or explain why the patient is in the hospital. They become so caught up in irrelevant details that they fail to see the big picture. I love to challenge interns and residents to tell me about each of their patients in just two sentences. Focus on the real problems at hand, the life-threatening problems. Details are abundant—but knowing which are relevant is what will truly set you apart. Life, like a patient presentation, is no different. Seeing the trees is easy. Seeing the forest is challenging.

Ants and Elephants

One personal story comes to mind when I think of seeing the big picture. My future wife and I were in the final stages of planning our dream wedding. Two Italian families. Strong opinions. Major investments. We had settled on an amazing, fancy hotel with a breathtaking ballroom. Every room in the hotel was gorgeous, each had its own character and history. While we were able to schedule our reception in the great ballroom, we were disappointed to learn that we were unable to book breakfast for our guests the next morning in our preferred room. I was not happy. My wife was not happy. My mother wasn't happy. My wife's mother wasn't happy. We all fueled one another's frustration and anger and lost sight of what was truly important as we planned the wedding.

Later that week, my dad, often the voice of reason, called to check in. I told him how upset we all were that we could not have the room we preferred. He listened patiently as I went on and on. His response was simple. "There are ants and there are elephants in this world. You will have a rough life if you can't differentiate between the two."

He was right. Most people in the world could only dream of having the wedding that we were so meticulously planning. Not one guest would ever know or care that their breakfast the morning after an amazing wedding would be in our second-choice room. Some would leave before breakfast, some would be too hungover to come, and some would just be happy to have food. It was an ant in the jungle of wedding planning. The consequence of the room change could be brushed aside, crushed with a shoe, and we could move on. The elephant was the wedding itself, the reason for the celebration.

Identifying what is important in life and what is irrelevant can bring a new level of both happiness and success to your career, relationships, and personal growth. It is not easy to start this new habit, but it will truly save you from unnecessary anxiety, frustration, and wasted energy.

So much of the world is focused on the minor, insignificant details, which often bombard the senses but have little effect on meaningful outcomes. Does it really matter that your car was scratched in the parking lot while you shopped at Target? That there is a stain on your beautiful new couch? How will this affect you four months from now? One year from now? Ten years from now? Ask this important question when you find yourself attempting to comprehend the significance of an event in life. If you were told that this was your last week on Earth, would this event mean anything to you? This helps put things into perspective and can help differentiate the meaningful events in life from the minutia. Building relationships, encouraging others, spending quality time with loved ones, counseling a friend—these are the important experiences in life. They live on beyond our existence. A car, a scratch, a stain? They are irrelevant. They are things, replaceable and always quick to fizzle away into the abyss of time. Learn to see the big picture. Do not be like a scared intern. Be a focused instructor.

The Man and the Construction Workers

There is another great story that illustrates the importance of understanding the big picture. You may have heard a version of it at some point.

A man was walking by a construction site one day and three men were working with wood scattered around a gravel clearing. The stranger approached the first man and asked him, "What is it that you are doing?" The worker replied, "I am measuring out this wood and making exact cuts, so the pieces fit into place perfectly." The man then approached the second worker and asked him the same question. He replied, "I am using this nail gun to fasten all the wood in place." When the stranger asked the third worker, "And what about you, sir, what is it that you are doing?" the worker replied with enthusiasm, "I am building a house!"

They were all doing the same thing, connecting the beams for the A-frame to make a roof. Yet only the third worker could see the big picture, not consumed with the details of his work. It is important to understand your role in the larger complexities of life and how this will fit into the result. This will add value to every task and more substance to every day.

The COVID-19 pandemic was eye opening for many people as it exposed the critical nature of certain jobs and how important they were in the overall function of our economy as well as the persistent wellbeing of the general population. It became noticeably clear that the person stocking the grocery store was in fact, incredible vital. They were not just putting items on a shelf; they were helping supply families with fresh food. They were helping to feed an entire nation.

Do Not Let Details Paralyze Your Plan of Action

During World War II, Winston Churchill, after hearing that the landing craft engineers were spending the majority of their time arguing over design changes, sent this message. "The maxim 'Nothing avails but perfection' may be spelt shorter: 'Paralysis.'

Being attentive to detail is good. Being overly and falsely attentive can be detrimental. Overanalyzing a situation, person, or a decision will sometimes lead to a pattern of indecisiveness, and derail progress or much needed changes.

I have seen quality physicians buckle under the pressure of having to make rapid and important clinical decisions. In medicine, especially critical care, every choice has a potential negative consequence. Life is no different. Do not spend eternity trying to find the perfect way to handle every situation. Perfection does not exist. Instead, learn to decipher which details are important and analyze the risks and benefits of each decision. This can take years to master, but if successful you will find both happiness and success sooner.

There are always risks in any decision or commitment. Consider and attempt to control the risks that are substantial and suppress the risks that are minimal. Do this in every aspect of your life and you will have less anxiety, a heightened mood, more free time, and confidence to succeed.

Avoiding "analysis paralysis" is a hot topic in self-help circles. I encourage you to take some time to explore this topic further in your pursuit of your career and improving relationships.

The 80 / 20 Rule

Our time on Earth is limited, and how we chose to prioritize it will ultimately determine both our level of success and happiness. I can't begin to tell you how many times I have heard medical students or classmates through the years say, "I studied so hard, but I still did terrible on that test." See, most of these people, even myself on many occasions, made the fatal mistake of focusing on quantity rather than quality. Long hours of work and preparation will do no good if they are spent on the wrong task.

As I pursued my education beyond high school, I learned what usually determined whether I did well on a certain exam. It was not *how* long I studied, but *where* I focused most of my time. For example, I realized at a young age that mathematics was just not my strong suit. Specifically, I struggled with statistics. I spent endless hours before the MCAT trying to understand the nuances of the subject; terms like *autoregressive integrated moving average*. The percentage of statistics on the MCAT is small, and is out of balance with the time I spent preparing for that topic. Had I understood where to effectively use my time, perhaps my MCAT score would have been better.

After that, I refused to spend any time studying statistics as I prepared for board exams.

Statistics will always be a part of medicine, yet it is a small part—and for me, not worth throwing away hours of time to learn. Small decisions such as this helped me perform immensely better on standardized testing moving forward. Pathophysiology was medicine. Statistics was just a tool in my education. Statistics was the tree, but pathophysiology was the forest.

This is not a new, unique concept, but one preached by business leaders, elite athletes, and other successful people all over the world. It is sometimes referred to as the Pareto principle. It states that 80% of effects come from 20% of the causes. The idea was first recognized and made famous by Vilfredo Pareto in the late 1800s, who observed that 80% of the land in Italy was owned by 20% of the population. [16] In sales, they say that 20% of clients provide 80% of the income. [17] In baseball, 15% of the players with the top WAR (win above replacement) produced 85% of the wins.[18] It's not entirely true to say that this simple rule of thumb can be applied to *every* aspect of life. However, it reveals the importance of identifying where to funnel energy in order to remain more efficient and effective.

How to Better See the Forest

1. Understand that your time is precious. Minimizing waste on minor, irrelevant details will prevent you from reaching your full potential. Focus your energy on lasting causes, not material things that are replaceable. Delegate when possible in order to spend time on tasks that you excel at and enjoy.

2. Set goals every month. You should have two to three sets of goals you set every month. One should be for your personal life, such as exercising for a certain amount of time. One should pertain to your career, and how you can better yourself and become more valuable to your profession or your job. The third goal applies to those in relationships or married, and should focus on a joint goal, such as eating dinner as a family every night. By making goals we train our minds to differentiate what is relevant, and it helps us learn to focus on efficiently accomplishing important things. It is common knowledge that you are much more likely to achieve success if you set realistic goals.

3. Utilize the 80/20 rule. To help improve our personal wellbeing we can identify those aspects of our life that either have the largest negative impact, or the potential to have the greatest positive impact. This helps us more easily and efficiently transform our life. The same concept also works for our careers, as well as personal relationships with our spouse, friends, or other family members. For example, it is safe to say many of the disagreements or arguments between my spouse and I revolve around the same few topics. Discussing, negotiating, and improving in these areas has led to a significant reduction in friction, thus improving our marriage. This type of intervention can be applied to most relationships, not limited to just marriage.

Richard Koch, author of the book *The 80/20 Rule,* summed up this concept well, stating, "If we realized the difference between the vital few and the trivial many in all aspects of our lives, and if we did something about it, we could multiply anything we valued."

Building a smile starts with seeing the forest through the trees.

Chapter 5: Find Your Light (In and at the End of the Tunnel)

"In the middle of difficulty, lies opportunity."

- Albert Einstein

On many days, life is like traveling through a tunnel. Dark, cold, lonely, with no way out. We barrel forward, get through our specific tasks, and never tap our full potential, because we have lost the excitement to do so. Some days things do not go our way. Sometimes our dream job bores us, our loved ones drive us up the wall, and we struggle to smile.

The Power of Pleasure

The unique challenge of each day is what makes life so exciting, yet for many people the challenge is what deters them from obtaining joy. Fortunately, our amazing brains have evolved through years of human tragedy and despair. Every member of our gene pool has survived because they had the tools to overcome difficult and uninteresting situations. Besides altering our perception of the world, as discussed in the previous chapters, there is another instrument to help us maintain happiness and positivity. Establishing and anticipating a specific desired event or activity every day will help guide you through the rough days. This is also known as *future mental time travel* and is a unique ability of the human mind.

We all have certain things in life that we enjoy: a specific TV show, cooking dinner, playing an instrument, working out, playing a sport, being intimate with a significant other, going on vacation. It does not matter what you love to do in life. Enjoying things in life is easy. It's innate. We are born with certain preferences, and we feel gratification. It is HOW we use what we love in life to better ourselves and bring happiness every day that is important. That is the real concept to grasp. The utilization of harmless gratification is a powerful motivator. A keyword here is "harmless." Getting inebriated every night to escape reality is not a tool, it is a destructive force. I doubt most people need a lecture on what is good or bad for them. I will save that for another author more qualified to discuss such a topic.

Every day when I wake up, I try to immediately identify something that night to look forward to. Most days I do not need to refer to it in order to get through the day. However, like a happiness pill in my back pocket, I have the anticipation of a gratifying event tucked away in my arsenal. It can be something simple—a steak dinner or favorite take out. Some days it is a movie or show my wife and I will watch. Sometimes it is a glass of wine, working in the garden, and playing the guitar. Whatever you love in life, I recommend using it to help cope with a challenging day.

What we love is a personal choice, variable across humanity. But the ability to use the anticipation of our personal enjoyments is a consistent option for all. The idea of identifying and anticipating a pleasurable event (future mental time travel) has carried me through many difficult times. An example of a specific challenge comes to mind: my internal medicine residency.

In my second year, there was a particularly difficult month, with four straight weeks of night coverage. I truly disliked doing night shift. The awkward meal schedule, difficulty exercising, feelings of solitude, and overall unhealthy situation made it a real challenge. I knew that to get through this month, I would need to find some sort of light at the end of the tunnel. It came in the form of a cheap diner meal and 20 minutes of privacy to read the local newspaper, every morning when my shift ended. It was the perfect cure to my challenging month. I realized the power of this tool during that tough block on my schedule, and I have used it ever since.

A Bit More about Future Mental Time Travel

The term "future mental time travel" is also known as *episodic future thinking*. Think of it as daydreaming but with focus and intent. It is defined by the ability to mentally project oneself forward in time to imagine an event from one's potential, personal future. This ability to imagine the future usually evolves from past experiences, and for most humans, episodic future thinking takes on a positive tone. In fact, evidence shows that many of these future thoughts are biased toward an overly positive self-image and exaggerated perception of self-control. [19]

An article from *the Journal of Positive Psychology* found that there was a significant increase in happiness for subjects when they used future mental time travel. It was postulated that positive future mental time travel could provide a new approach in happiness-boosting and stress-reducing activities. Maybe it could even be another option of behavior therapy for anxiety or depression? It's theorized that this unique ability is actually an evolutionary adaptive strategy of the human mind, and it helps us continue to seek out new opportunities and social relationships despite the real possibility of failure and disappointment.[20] The amount of research in this field is growing, and I would encourage readers to spend some time reviewing the literature, as it is fascinating.

For the purpose of this book, future mental time travel gives humans the rare ability to better cope with the present and achieve great success in the future by helping us visualize a specific goal and giving us active comfort in the present moment, utilizing some sort of gratifying event in the future.

We see practical evidence of this when people plan and take vacations. Do you know that feeling of excitement when you are planning a vacation? The fun in browsing details on different hotels and excursions, the anticipation as you pack your bags and head to the airport? Even waiting in the line for coffee in Terminal C feels a little bit different. A 2014 study at Cornell University found that people experience more happiness just knowing that they will be going on a vacation in the future. And even when compared to actual material spending, people seem to value the anticipation of an enjoyable experience more.[21] In other words, we find much more enjoyment when planning an experience (for example, a vacation) compared to planning the purchase of a material item (buying a car). This is no surprise, since humans are social beings programmed to value what is crucial to their social existence for years to come.

Another study done by professors at the University of Surrey echoed this concept. They found that individuals waiting to go on vacation are much happier with their life, experience fewer negative or unpleasant feelings, and enjoy more pleasant feelings. Researchers found that this group was also more content with their economic, family, and health domains compared with the non-vacation taking group.[22]

Anticipation of something positive also has a powerful impact in the business world, as a study from *the Journal of Industrial Relations* found. In this study, workers who believed a promotion was possible in the next two years reported much higher job satisfaction.[23] The simple act of giving employees a degree of "hope" could make them happier with their current situation, likely in the form of visualizing their future advancement within the company.

Powerful and clear, there is now practical and concrete evidence to support the notion that humans depend on a degree of positive future mental time travel to better deal with life challenges as well as placing continued value on social opportunities.

How to Light Your Tunnel

1. Daily visualization. Identify your daily "light at the end of the tunnel" when you wake up every morning. Pull it out of your pocket and refer to it whenever you are feeling overwhelmed, frustrated, or tired of how your day is going. Try to make a habit of using this anticipation as a tool to be happier. Every morning wake up and plan your daily vacation. Every night after the workday you can set sail.

2. Plan a trip. It does not need to be expensive, just something and somewhere enjoyable. Take time to plan the details and take enjoyment in the process.

3. Use positive mental time travel to your advantage. It is another unique ability of the human brain, might as well use it.

Building a smile starts with identifying your light at the end of the tunnel. Everyday.

Chapter 6: Don't Take it Personally

"The world is a magical place waiting for people to be offended by something."

—Anonymous

We must acknowledge today that we live in a hypersensitive society. It is an environment breeding intolerance, despite efforts to do the opposite. Lately, it seems near impossible to have real conversations about race, sexism, financial equality, and other sometimes-polarizing subjects because people may fear the consequences of having such dialogue. Say the wrong word, and someone may be offended or misinterpret your opinion. Do not say enough and you are labelled a coward for not standing up for a cause.

There is a large percentage of the population so obsessed with the opinions of others that they become imprisoned by the thoughts of someone else instead of moved to succeed through confidence in themselves. They dwell on every word of others, meticulously analyzing the meaning and intent of every syllable. We have a choice everyday whether we want to give in to the opinions of others or "thicken our skin" and push forward in life. Remember that people who are weak will use words to try to belittle others, while the strong will use action to strengthen us all.

To again quote Ben Franklin, "Words may show a man's wit but actions his meaning." Words are easy to speak. Take to heart what people do more so than what they say, and you will save yourself a substantial amount of grief. And even if they do things that you might not like, don't be offended. It's not about you, don't make things about you when they aren't, and look at the whole pattern of someone's actions before letting them hurt you.

What Is Your Emotional Type?

You have probably heard the term "thin-skinned," describing someone who is sensitive to criticism, opposing opinions, or insults. The opposite is to be thick-skinned. Psychoanalyst and sleep researcher Ernest Hartmann did extensive research in this field and he developed the theory known as *boundaries of the mind*. His theory stemmed from observing that people who suffer frequent nightmares had distinctive personality characteristics described as "unguarded," and "vulnerable." His work went on to classify individuals as either having thick boundaries or thin boundaries. Thin-boundary-emotion-type individuals become stressed or fatigued due to an overload of sensory or emotional input. Thick-boundary people tend to brush aside emotional upset in favor of "handling" the situation. Thin-boundary individuals were more likely to have certain psychiatric illnesses, such as depression and anxiety; and thick-boundary people had other chronic health issues like hypertension and heart disease. [24] It seems some of the chronic health issues that burden humans find roots in how we chose to deal with emotional challenges. For example, thick boundary individuals likely "bottle-up" feelings, leading to internal stress which manifests itself in long term physiological strain.

How Would You Classify Yourself? Does Any of This Really Matter?

We cannot really change our emotional boundary type. It's the way that we were born, from an emotional standpoint. I do, however, believe there is value in recognizing who we are and reflecting on ourselves in order to better manage our tendencies; either being hypersensitive to what others say and do or becoming cold and numb to our surroundings. The world we live in is full of social, economic, and career challenges. Knowing yourself from an emotional standpoint will give you a major advantage.

In a perfect world, changing the "thickness" of your skin depending on the situation is likely the best approach. If you chose to read through social media newsfeeds, it will pay to thicken your skin some. In deep interpersonal relationships, such as that with your significant other, it may be better to let more in and increase sensitivity or emotional expression. Adaptation of emotion is powerful and will help you more effectively cope with challenges.

Why Are We So Sensitive?

I believe there are three main reasons our society has become hypersensitive, dominated by people taking anything and everything way too personally.

1. Low Self-Esteem and Fear of Rejection

Increasing members of society, especially our youth, seem to be lacking an adequate self-esteem. For example, on social media, people often compare themselves to bogus Instagram pictures and exaggerated vacation posts, and they tend to lose self confidence in themselves. They begin to feel inferior, less content with their own lives, and naturally have trouble gaining confidence. When we lack self-esteem, we do not have the capability to withstand critique. Adequate self-confidence is key to both success and sustained happiness. Build yourself up so the world has a harder time pushing you down.

2. Everyone Wins in This New World

As a society, we seem to be sheltering our youth to serve our own feelings rather than focusing on raising a strong generation of children. A maturing individual needs to feel fear, embarrassment, and inferiority. They need to sit in the corner and soak in a loss or critique. They need to get made fun of occasionally. This is how they become prepared for the real world. In our current world, we are at risk of raising a group of weak, hypersensitive individuals if we continue to shelter them from feeling left out. When we overprotect children, we are not arming them with the coping skills to confront life with strength. I would never support bullying, though there seems to be a thin line we are navigating as a society and careful attention should be paid to better building a foundation of tolerance in our youth.

3. We Are Normalizing Intolerance

Examples of sensitivity gone array and intolerance are everywhere. Politicians are refusing to debate certain topics or attempt to use their position to suppress others opinions, simply because they do not agree. While I recognize we must always tolerate, even the intolerant, maintaining the ability for society to have constructive discussions on challenging topics must remain a priority.

A well done op-ed written by Rachel Huebner, published in *the Harvard Crimson*, does a great job highlighting this point. She describes the current culture on college campuses as defined not by open expression, but by sensitivity. Perhaps the best example came from the author's own classroom experience. While establishing rules for the semester, a female student in one class stated that she would refuse to sit across any student that opposed abortion. The entire class approved, and the professor remained silent. [25] If society is encouraging us to not even look at people we disagree with, how will a generation of young adults learn to resolve conflicts and progress as a society?

How Sensitive Are You?

What emotions do you feel when someone does not agree with you? How do you feel after you find out you were not invited to an event, included in an email, or part of a major decision at work? How about when someone you invite to an event does not attend? How much energy do you spend per day worrying about what other people think about you? Do you find yourself asking *Is he or she mad at me? Did I say something wrong?*

These questions are likely to stir up negative feelings, but also sound quite familiar for many of us. That is OK. It's to be expected. We all strive for acceptance and that is normal. How we cope with being left out, worrying about rejection, and not being treated fairly, however, is what will determine our state of mind moving forward. We all must learn to not take things so personally.

Let's look at some ways to improve how we cope with some of the challenges posed in these questions.

1. Understand That Disagree and Dislike Are Two Vastly Different Things. It is vital to recognize that people will many times disagree with you in life. Disagreements are what lead to progress and compromise, bringing two or more differing ideas together—hopefully, the best of each. The Founding Fathers spent months disagreeing about how to build the United States. It was the differing opinions of the men in that room that built our great republic. Sometimes colleagues and I disagree about the management of a patient, yet it is our discussion that will undoubtedly lead to the best care. Emotionally immature individuals will feel anger when hearing the differing opinions of others, or critical remarks in regard to their own views. This in turn often spirals into people believing others do not like them simply because they do not agree with them. Let me be clear: you will marinade in anger on many days unless you can mature into embracing some opinions and advice while learning to ignore others. Emotionally mature people will engage with people that have a different upbringing or a different opinion and will embrace criticism; ultimately growing from every disagreement. Mahatma Gandhi said it best: "Honest disagreement is often a good sign of progress."

2. Learn How to Develop a Thick Skin and Develop Your Self-Confidence. This starts when you stop fearing the rejection of others and accepting that sometimes certain people may not like you. That is OK. That is life. If you have developed your self-esteem appropriately, this can be ignored. Why do you care if someone doesn't like you? If you believe in yourself, then you know that it is in fact their loss, not yours.

Eleanor Roosevelt said, "No one can make you feel inferior without your consent." Do not become dependent on others to build up your self-esteem. For long-term happiness and success, you must have the tools and understanding to sit in a room, look in a mirror, and convince the person you see glaring back at you that you are, in fact, great. Life coach and bestselling author Rob Liano reiterated this narrative, saying, "Self-respect, self-worth, and self-love, all start with *self*. Stop looking outside yourself for your value."

By gaining more self-confidence, you will gain the ability to not take things so personally, because you will not seek the approval of others. The only approval you need is your own. This will allow the best of who you are to shine through.

The foundation of building a high self-esteem starts with bettering yourself. Only you can take control of who you are and who you strive to be in the future. Constantly try to educate yourself, accept new challenges to allow for more accomplishments, exercise your mind and body as often as possible, treat others with respect, and stay humble. The results will be profound.

3. Accept Reality. Accept Being Left Out. Remember in life that you cannot be invited to every place, every time. For example, think about when you have had to make difficult decisions and edit a guest list for an event. It's challenging. You sometimes end up feeling bad, but the reality is that you cannot invite your entire network of friends to every event. Accept that others cannot do it, either. Beyond missing out on events, you are going to be left out many times in life. You will inevitably feel as though the world is against you. Do not worry. This is not true. Do not take it personally. Don't make it about you. In fact, in certain circumstance realize that it can be best to grace people with your absence. Author and motivational speaker Steve Maraboli said: "Every time I thought I was being rejected from something good, I was actually re-directed to something better." Embrace rejection as an opportunity to embark on a new venture or experience in life.

4. Understand Your Emotional Sensitivities. As mentioned earlier, understanding your emotional sensitivities will allow you to acknowledge when you are perhaps being oversensitive. When this happens, you can take a minute, step back from the situation, and reassess the appropriateness of how you are feeling.

In the end, rise above the opinions, differences, and critiques of others. The best version of yourself starts with the maturity and strength to stand out by not being offended. Be different by not caring so much when the time is right.

Building a smile starts with not taking things so personally.

Chapter 7: Forgive and Move On

"To forgive is to set a prisoner free and discover that the prisoner was you."

–Lewis B. Smedes

Perhaps the most famous story of forgiveness comes from the Bible; the parable of the prodigal son in Luke 15. A father had two sons. His youngest son begged his father to receive his inheritance early, and his father eventually agreed. The son then went to a faraway land, going on to spend all the money and taking part in foolish and sinful activities. Not long after, a famine swept the land and he was forced to work in the fields, often eating the animal slop as he was so hungry and poor. One day he decided he could suffer no more and he returned to his father's home to ask for forgiveness and help.

When the man arrived at his father's property, he was deeply ashamed. So, he was surprised to see his father run toward him, then embrace and kiss him. The son said, "Father, I have sinned against heaven and in your sight, and am no longer worthy to be called your son."

The father replied by calling to his servants, "Bring out the best robe and put it on him and put a ring on his hand and sandals on his feet. And bring the fatted calf here and kill it, and let us eat and be merry; for this my son was dead and is alive again; he was lost and is found."

How many times has someone hurt you or betrayed you like the son in the above story did to his father? Have there been situations when you were reluctant to let people back in your life? This father knew that his son was in pain due to his betrayal, therefore his eagerness to be truthful and learn from his past mistakes was celebrated.

Imperfection and Mortality

One hundred percent of you reading this book will perish from this Earth. Sixty percent of those currently living in the US will die in a hospital, and many of those individuals will pass through the ICU (intensive care unit) at some point in their last month of life. Though I have been blessed with great fortune in my lifetime, my work as a critical care physician has often placed me incredibly close to life's final chapter.

Every life is different, and every death unique. Some final hours are peaceful with loved ones offering support; some are painful and lonely. Some people fight death, while others accept it. It is sometimes planned, and other times comes unannounced. No matter the life lived, as humans, it is a guarantee: we will leave this Earth at some point, and we will do so imperfectly. Like death, our mistakes also come in many forms; sometimes for the world to see, other times tucked away in the comfort of our private life. Sometimes our errors are accepted, sometimes unaccepted and fought against. But like death, our imperfections and wrongdoings will always present themselves at some point. If we can accept these two facts, we will each live a fuller life.

Theoretical physicist and cosmologist Stephen Hawking was quick to acknowledge the concept of imperfection, saying, "One of the basic rules of the universe is that nothing is perfect. Perfection simply doesn't exist. Without imperfection, neither you nor I would exist."

The faster we learn to embrace this idea that life is finite, and we are each imperfect, the more quickly and effectively we can forgive ourselves and the people that surround each of us. This seems especially difficult for younger individuals, where a feeling of immortality and flawlessness often prevails. Realizing that you are not invincible at a young age will pay dividends. People will lie to you, cheat on you, talk about you behind your back, and attempt to bring you down. Sometimes the people closest with you will hurt you the most. This is the course in life. We can accept the consequences of humanity or we can fight an unwinnable battle for perfection.

Accepting that we are imperfect enables us to look beyond the flaws or wrongdoings of others, knowing that we too are capable of such mistakes. By accepting that life is finite, we can better appreciate that there is truly no time to waste on holding grudges. Perhaps it is best said by author Dave Willis in his book *The Seven Laws of Love*: "Holding a grudge doesn't make you strong; it makes you bitter. Forgiving does not make you weak; it sets you free."

Eliminate Grudges

Still, many people in this world hold lifelong grudges. Something that happened 30 years ago somehow remains relevant. Like a smoker trying to kick their habit, ridding ourselves of these feelings only gets more difficult with time. Sometimes these grudges are the result of a simple argument or disagreement, a public embarrassment, or a misinterpretation of words. Other times, the resentment comes from deeper and more serious occurrences.

Philosopher Eckhart Tolle perhaps best captured the importance of releasing those grudges in his book *The Power of Now*. He states, "Most people need to experience a great deal of suffering before they will relinquish resistance and accept, before they will forgive." Once people do forgive a great miracle occurs, the "awakening of being-consciousness through what appears as evil, the transmutation of suffering into inner peace." He goes on to explain that without forgiveness, evil persists with no opposite in sight, and that forgiveness essentially means that we recognize the insubstantiality of the past. [26]

I think this concept is especially important to grasp and is powerful if conquered. Reflecting on the past has its role, yet many times we seem to overestimate its importance. A key component of forgiveness and moving on is understanding the insignificance of many past events.

Forgive Yourself and Eliminate Guilt

Although we often find it challenging to forgive others, it is in fact more difficult to forgive ourselves.

I am no stranger to the burden of guilt. An Italian Catholic upbringing with relatively strict parents set the stage for a life of constant self-reflection and often second-guessing my previous actions or feelings.

Guilt does not always have to be felt towards something "big." This may sound ridiculous, but I often felt guilty when I was not working. My parents ingrained into each of their kids a strong work ethic, an expectation to work hard in all aspects of life. I carried this with me into adulthood, and while it has certainly pushed me to succeed, there are times I carry it as a burden, "I must be lazy," I would think to myself. This sometimes prevented me from enjoying time off. Believe it or not, something so ridiculous caused me major distress. After years of carrying this weight, I came to the realization that there was no wrongful act done by resting, and that these feelings were counterproductive to my happy state of mind. I came to understand the heavy burden of what often felt like insignificant guilt.

On the contrary, I often hear parents stating that they feel guilty for working, as they struggle with the emotions tied to not being home and spending time with their children. The reality is, that in today's world, it often takes the income of two parents to provide enough to live comfortably. Never allow the feeling of guilt complicate the desire to provide for your family, as this very notion is counter intuitive and counterproductive by nature.

While sometimes difficult to swallow, guilt is a necessary emotion, often initiating empathy, understanding, and acknowledgement of wrongdoing. However, like everything else in life, too much of anything can become destructive. Author Sabaa Tahir appropriately summed this up, saying, "There are two kinds of guilt: the kind that drowns you until you're useless, and the kind that fires your soul to purpose." For me, feeling guilty for not working became destructive. Let guilt be the spark that makes you a better human, not the 100lb boulder that pulls you to the bottom of the sea.

The first step to ridding yourself of guilt is to forgive yourself for any wrongdoing. Refer to the earlier part of this chapter about the two guarantees—we are all imperfect and life is finite. Self-reflect and self-forgive. No one is perfect;

including you. Good people say and do bad things. This is the nature of humanity.

Next, differentiate between appropriate or productive guilt and counterproductive guilt. Appropriate guilt, for example, sounds like, "I was dishonest with my significant other." This type of guilt is valuable because it will help you recognize what you did wrong and help you prevent it from happening again. It will make you a better person by urging you to action. The key to utilizing productive guilt is to be sure to resolve it with conversation and honest attempts at altering how you live your life. Let everything be a lesson in how to better yourself. Do not leave guilt unresolved and carry the burden with you in silence and inaction, as this will be detrimental to your wellbeing. The act of "moving on" may require action, conversation and acceptance.

An example of counterproductive guilt is "I didn't express my love to my mother before she passed away or become very ill." As a critical care physician, I see this often. This type of guilt is powerful and potentially detrimental. It drives humans to make irrational decisions to correct the past, far too late to have any real impact. It is useless in the fact that it is not resolvable and often inaccurate. Accept that you are not perfect, rectify any wrongdoing with your loved ones, and move on. Times of great stress and change such as death, marriage, divorce, and career transitions often elicit strong emotions, and guilt tends to be one of the more common. Controlling this emotion will help you better deal with these sometimes-challenging chapters in your life.

The Power of Forgiveness

Learn the art of forgiveness, and you will open endless doors of potential and achieve a more consistent state of wellbeing. Forgiveness often reduces both short- and long-term confrontation, freeing both yourself and others of negativity and allowing you more free time to be productive in a finite life. There is evidence that forgiveness can also have lasting impact on our long term health; improving cardiovascular function, reducing chronic pain and even improving compliance with drug rehab programs. [27]

Forgiving others gives you power, as you will be viewed as strong, resilient, and caring. Others will look up you and envy your ability, even if they speak ill of you in the process. Forgiving others inherently allows more acceptance of your own flaws and mistakes, which is crucial in reducing guilt, staying humble, and improving your outlook in life. Forgiveness helps lift the burden of hate from the world, as it is the ultimate weapon to help humanity overcome evil and imperfection.

How can we better forgive others?

1. Remember the two important points we mentioned earlier in the chapter: Life is finite and we are all imperfect. This is the foundation of forgiveness.
2. Understand that the past cannot be changed.
3. Comprehend that the past is often insignificant.
4. Learn to first forgive ourselves.

Building a smile starts with forgiving others and forgiving yourself.

Chapter 8: Find Your Purpose, Pursue Your Passion

"The two most important days in your life are the day you were born and the day you find out why."

–Mark Twain

Why are you on this Earth today? Will you fall asleep tonight fulfilled in your daily actions? What gives you the most satisfaction in life? The answers to these questions are likely complex, confusing, and unique to every individual reading or listening to this book. This is what makes life great. Not only are we all so different, each of our roles on Earth is also incredibly diverse. Traversing this diversity of purpose can be challenging, but if successful; you will live your life through a brand-new lens of clarity and positivity.

Everyone has a purpose. Even a criminal serving a life sentence has a role. Perhaps he can serve as an example of the consequences of bad decisions to young kids living on the streets in crime-ridden neighborhoods. Even more important, after self-forgiveness and understanding, he could possibly influence another prisoner in a positive way; going on to help someone turn their life around for the better. The purpose of professional athletes is to entertain and to be positive role models to our youth, the purpose of a physician is to heal the ill and comfort their loved ones, and the purpose of a politician is to lead and articulate the desires of the people. A place for purpose is everywhere, and in anything.

As you move through jobs, careers, and passions, it is important to never lose sight of this concept.

Job, Career, and Passion

It is important to clarify some nomenclature that is often misunderstood. A job, a career, and a passion are all different things, yet all very much connected. A *job* is specific work you are paid to perform. You may have many jobs in your life, some short term and others longer term; all with differing compensation and expectations. A *career* is a lifelong journey within a specific profession. My career is medicine, and my current job is critical-care physician. A *passion* is something much deeper.

Let's try to understand the differences between a career and a passion. A career, in the form of a specific job, is what earns money to keep the lights glowing, food on the table, and the Amazon packages coming. A passion is what excites you to get out of bed each morning. A career has clear daily and long-term objectives, many times with a reward for a certain achievement. A passion is always rewarding, despite the stage of development. A career many times requires training or education. A passion often involves unconditional enjoyment and love, no matter the level of expertise.

For example, my wife went to nursing school and eventually found her way into the field of plastic surgery and cosmetic procedures. Throughout her journey, there was always one constant love, one clear passion. When she used to work in the hospital, she spent many of her days off taking family portraits for anyone interested. She received a small payment for her work, but that was never the motivation.

She had a genuine love for photography. At every stage of her relationship with this field, she found enjoyment, and while it involved hard work, it never felt like a burden to her.

Eventually, her love for photography infiltrated into her new job and she now spends hours taking and editing "before and after" pictures of her procedures. Much of her free time is spent filtering through photographs and utilizing content to build her portfolio, educate patients, and advertise special events. She does not get paid for this, but her love of photography found its way into her current job and career and it has significantly improved her job performance and satisfaction.

Most individuals have a job, many individuals have a career of some sort, some have a passion, the lucky few have a career which incorporates their passion.

Passion, Hobby, and Dreams

Realizing your passion can be a lifelong pursuit, or a quick awakening at an early age. Either way the results and satisfaction can be the same, as the pursuit itself can be rewarding. For me, it took some time, but there was great joy every step of the way. Like most people my age, I developed many enjoyments over the years: cooking, playing the guitar, playing golf, watching football. It was tempting on many days, as I fell in love with activities like these, to declare one day that they were my passion. "I got it! I want to be a professional golfer because I just love playing golf!" Or I would want to be a celebrity chef or the next famous rock star. These are great hobbies, and it never hurts to give it a shot. But I want to caution against being fooled into mistaking a hobby you love for a passion or career.

Another unfortunate mistake is the irrational decision to pursue a dream camouflaged as a passion or career. The singer that cannot sing is fighting a losing battle. The sprinter that runs slowly will lose many races. Certain dreams require real talent, and we can potentially waste a life of potential if we do not acknowledge our own limitations and the talents that we do have. Accomplishing this can take a degree of humility and self-reflection, but it will pay dividends in terms of future success and happiness. I am not here to crush your dreams; I am here to divert them into something which is attainable. Embrace your talents and abilities, and use them to formulate a career and attain a passion that makes it a pleasure to wake up every day.

Finding My Passion

I always felt that I probably could have been happy doing most things in life. I ran a landscaping business through high school and part of college. I also worked for a small deli making sandwiches and worked at a motel at the front desk checking customers in and answering phone calls. These jobs helped develop my interests and added a new skill set: talking to people. Sometimes terribly angry people. I was happy in each of these ventures, and each position helped, in some way, to lead me to the present moment.

Through the years, as I developed my skills as a critical care physician, I have had the honor of sharing some of the most difficult times a family or person will face. Severe illness and the immediate threat of death changes people's lives immediately. It changes the patient's life for obvious reasons, but it also forever alters those that surround their loved one in those difficult days. More often than you could imagine, I get the same question from distressed family members. "How can you do this every day?"

I think about that question often. I think about it especially when young students ask me for career advice. It's through these conversations with struggling families that I have finally come to realize my passion in life. It took me five years into my career before I had an understanding. It took time. I realize now that helping families and people cope with difficult news and supporting them through challenging end-of-life decisions is the most rewarding job on the planet. It is at times exhausting, terribly sad, and painful, but always worth the price. It challenges me every day and fulfills me just the same.

Of course, I share a similar love for medicine and the human body, as its capabilities and complexities amaze me every day. It was my infatuation with physiology while taking a course in undergraduate school that truly sparked my interest in pursuing medicine. My early understanding and love for physiology lead me to my career, which in turn lead me to my passion. But if you dig deeper, my passion had always existed. It followed me during my time working in the hotel and deli, through my education, and every step of my career. My passion is people—comforting them, learning from them, listening to them, and sometimes leading them. My role in guiding patients and families through their most difficult days and leading other physicians through the complicated world of healthcare lets me utilize my passion every day. How can I do this every day? How could I not.

Through time my other passions have evolved, including, more recently, the joy of writing. Medicine has allowed me unique life experience and perspective, and part of my goal and calling in life is to share this with the world.

It is not perfect, the path to the so-called promised land of the ideal blend of career and passion. Everything worth anything in life takes sacrifice, determination, patience, and hard work; and the journey of a career path is no different. While often difficult to predict and sometimes rough on the soul, in many ways this pursuit can be equally as enjoyable as the accomplishment. I enjoyed every step along the way as I added the building blocks of my career and the puzzle pieces of my passion. The journey has allowed me to travel, live in different states and far-away countries, and meet amazing people.

If you make the best of every job you take and every educational challenge you pursue, find enjoyment in everything you do, constantly attempt to better yourself, and always plan the next move in an effort to better your position; you too will find the same pleasure. You too will slowly come to realize your passion, as you move back and forth through the ever-changing labyrinth of career and education.

Finding passion within your career will exalt you to new heights with almost no real strenuous effort. It will allow you to give every bit of yourself, all while finding enjoyment in the process. Dale Carnegie, author of the timeless, bestselling book *How to Win Friends and Influence People,* articulated the importance of giving it your all, stating, "The average person puts only 25% of his energy into his work. The world takes off its hat to those who put in more than 50% of their capacity, and stands on its head for those few and far between souls who devote 100%."

It is never too late to try to become the rare individual who has passion for their career and is eager to give 100% of themselves. If you do these two things, your life will take on a new meaning.

Understand your purpose, find your love, connect it to a career that can provide for you, and be willing to take a risk while doing so. For example, if you have a love for graphic design, ask your boss if you can be a part of the website development team or making brochures, even if it is not within your department. If your passion is writing, offer to start an employee newsletter or blog. Offer to do it for free and show your value and ambition. Do not expect compensation in the early stages as you find your way. The money will come, and new career opportunities will be plentiful. I promise. This is the key. Identify your love and begin applying it to your current job and let it open doors to new ventures. You will be surprised how often this is possible.

In the words of Swiss philosopher Henri Frederic Amiel, "Without passion man is a mere latent force and possibility, like the flint which awaits the shock of the iron before it can give forth its spark."

Building a smile starts with understanding your purpose and pursuing your passion.

Chapter 9: Disconnect

"There is something beautiful about not knowing everything about everyone."

-Robert M. Cole

Stop reading or listening to this book and think about your average cell phone screen time over the last week. If you're anything like me, you will be astonished by the amount of time wasted per day on this tiny device. I do not mean just texting, emailing for work, or conference calls. Look at the time you spend on news apps, mindless games, Instagram, Facebook, Twitter, TikTok, and Snapshot. You are not alone in your excessive phone use. Worldwide, the average person uses their cell phone for 3.1 hours per day, about a quarter of their waking hours. [28]

Nothing in history has changed the way humans communicate more than the advent of the internet and cell phones. In fact, we are still in the beginning stages of understanding how this has changed how we connect forever. Beyond basic communication, the introduction of social media has allowed everyone's thoughts to be viewed by millions—immediately. It has allowed for instant feedback, unfiltered and unchecked. Unfortunately, many of these platforms promote an exaggeration of success, the misperception of happiness, and often breed envy, jealousy, and hatred.

Is everything about a cell phone and social media negative? No. They have helped bring people together, raise money for good causes, helped us keep in touch with relatives, and added a new weapon to promote and run a business. This very book may be promoted on social media. The cell phone makes me a more efficient and effective physician on most days. The need for this technology is obvious, but it has come at a great, unclear cost of psychological illness, loss of time, and mounting evidence of an addiction.

Addicted and Depressed

Our cell phones have increasingly become a part of our every move, a constant distraction from our family and friends, always pulling us from the present moment. The more we use our phones, especially as we browse through social media apps, the more dopamine that is released in our brain, giving us a feeling of unnatural bliss. It has become obvious that we are all becoming addicts, one click or swipe at a time.

As I go through a typical day, I rarely find individuals who are truly present. Between checking and posting on social media and returning text messages or emails, most of us seem to live through a screen, cut off from reality. When a child says something adorable or (even better yet) hits a developmental milestone, what is our response? Convince them to say it or do it again so we can record the event. We never let the actual event soak in. We probably did not even pay attention, because we were scrambling to find our cellphone and turn on the camera. For some reason, it seems more important to record and share the event than to enjoy the actual moment. The absurdity is nauseating.

Recently, I witnessed a scary and outrageous example of phone addiction. For a quick getaway, my wife and I decided to take our toddler to the beach. As we waded in the cool ocean, I glanced over to the lifeguard stand. To my utter shock and disappointment, I saw two teenage boys staring at their cell phones. Both were looking down, oblivious to their surroundings. As dozens of young families were splashing and carrying on in front of them, relying on an extra layer of safety, these two young men found it more important to text their friends or check their Instagram account. Shocking. Disappointing. Sad. This is the new norm, the new world we live in. Few people are ever truly present anymore; they are consumed with a world attached to their hand.

But are these devices and apps really being built to keep us hooked? It seems the answer is yes. "Brain Hacking" is a term few people in the tech industry will say out loud. It is a phrase some programmers use when describing their efforts to keep users constantly feeling the need to check in with their smart phones. This was explained in a *60 Minutes* special with Tristan Harris, a former product manager for Google.

He compared a cell phone to a slot machine, explaining, "Every time I check my phone, I'm playing the slot machine to see, 'What did I get?' This is one way to hijack people's minds and create a habit, to form a habit. What you do is you make it so when someone pulls the lever, sometimes they get a reward, an exciting reward. And it turns out that this design technique can be embedded inside of all these products." He goes on to explain the rewards of picking up your phone include "likes" on Facebook and Instagram, emojis in text messages, and new followers on Twitter.

Larry Rosen, a psychiatrist from California State University Dominguez Hills, has studied the impact of cell phone use on the brain. In the same *60 Minutes* interview, he explained, "What we find is the typical person checks their phone every 15 minutes or less, and half of the time when they check their phone there is no alert, no notification. It's coming from inside their head, telling them, 'Gee, I haven't checked Facebook in a while. I haven't checked on this Twitter feed for a while. I wonder if somebody commented on my Instagram post.' That then generates cortisol, and it starts to make you anxious. And eventually your goal is to get rid of that anxiety, so you check in."[29]

In other words, cortisol, the powerful hormone which from an evolutionary perspective was developed to help us deal with the necessary fight-or-flight response when hunting or running from prey, is being constantly secreted at the mercy of our cell phone. Why could this be a bad thing? An abundance of cortisol causes increases in blood pressure and blood sugar, decreased immunity, can alter our mood and weaken our bone structure. The long-term health impacts of phone addiction and the constant release of dopamine and cortisol remain unclear.

In the HBO series, *Real Time with Bill Maher*, the host interestingly compared social media companies to the tobacco industry and the infusion of nicotine to make the products more addicting. Maher said, "Philip Morris just wanted your lungs, the app store wants your soul." In reference to our often-machine-tethered existence, Maher says, "Pedestrian deaths are way up because people in the crosswalks looking down are getting run over by drivers looking down. The whole damn world is looking down."

Much of the population is tangled in the addiction of texting and getting "likes" on social media like an alcoholic sipping a vodka and orange juice all day at work. Hidden in the downward gaze, many of us have become zombies to the real world, drunk to reality.

With this great power and potential of portable communication has come great responsibility to society, and great pain to many individuals. I feel strongly, from personal experience as well as through mounting evidence, that cell phone use and specifically the abuse of social media is changing, and in some ways, destroying the natural way we communicate. There is real concern that this is leading to greater depression, destroying self-esteem, and seriously handicapping the social skills of an entire generation of human beings.

Much of what people see on a social media post is an effort by individuals to manipulate how others view them, rather than a reflection of what is real. A picture of a happy family on the beach is a snapshot of reality. Few individuals will post that they lost their job or are now enrolled in marriage counseling, and because this is not being communicated, it gives the false perception that it does not exist. A frustrated adolescent might post a personal thought in a rage of anger or fear that has lifelong consequences, recorded permanently for the world to see. A bikini picture has been edited extensively to reveal a fake reality. No one has flawless skin. No one is perfect.

It is not surprising that there appears to be a robust correlation between increased screen time and increased depressive symptoms, suicide, and poor sleep habits; especially in adolescents and young adults. [30] I have little doubt any age group is spared these effects.

In addition, passive consumption of social media content, as opposed to active communication, has been associated with a decrease in bonding and bridging social capital and an increase in loneliness. [31] It is becoming clearer that gathering likes and reading a newsfeed stimulates dopamine in your brain in the same way that it does for gamblers playing games or drug addicts getting high. The irony of it all? Like every bad habit, most of us dislike social media . . . though we continue to use it at a breakneck pace. [32]

My Departure from the Social Media World

If mounting scientific evidence is not enough to convince you of the detrimental effects of social media abuse, take my advice based on personal experience. More than seven years ago I decided to permanently delete all social media applications and accounts. An awkward encounter with a complete stranger instigated this abrupt departure. This would end up being one of the best decisions of my life. Those that know me, know I am not shy in discussing this life change.

At first, I missed flipping through the feeds, viewing accounts, looking up people I met, and hearing odd opinions. There was, of course, a void at first, but soon that void was filled with productive behavior, a cleaner state of mind, and a more present existence.

Within just several days of being social media free I discovered a new sense of reality. It was as if the world changed just by eliminating one component of life. Ending one bad habit opened so many doors. Suddenly, I had hours of free time I could use to accomplish other goals. I gained about two hours per day of time, and that expanded out to seven years is net gain of 212 days, close to an extra year of life. Further calculate that out to a lifetime of 70 years, and I will have gained nearly six years! Beyond saving hours of time, this decision eliminated so much unnecessary anger, disappointment, and resentful feelings toward others. I no longer know the controversial personal opinions of others, so in turn it is impossible to have a negative view of a person or group of people before meeting them.

There is something beautiful about not knowing everything about everyone. I think this can make for stronger and more effective relationships and a happier you. By limiting certain knowledge, perhaps it can prevent the opportunity for resentful and angry feelings to bubble over and create unnecessary confrontation or conflict. The fact that you do not agree with someone on a deep religious or social belief is unimportant, just as long as that person is a good person, respectful to you and your family, and can help make a positive contribution to the world. It's not that you shouldn't care about other people, but do you really need to know what they had for dinner last night, where their dog pooped, what they are reading, and their deep and personal polarizing opinions? I feel it is better to develop a belief and discuss personal opinions in the form of an interactive conversation. I have little doubt this is a much healthier medium; a place where no one can hide behind the walls of a newsfeed.

Take the Challenge

Take a minute and ask yourself these important questions. On average, what is your daily screen time? (If you have an iPhone, it will track this information for you.) If you cut your screen time in half, how much time would that free up in a year? Have many of your relationships been ruined by interactions on social media? Do you develop strong opinions about people you have never even met? How do you feel as you browse? What would you do with your newly-found free time? Do you experience feelings such as jealousy, resentment, anger, frustration, and decrease in self-worth when browsing through newsfeeds or viewing other social media content?

Now accept my challenge and delete your social media apps for one week. Try extrapolating this out to other time-consuming behaviors on your phone, whether it is mindless games or browsing the news. Reassess after a week of screen time reduction. What have you accomplished with your free time? How do you feel?

I beg you to take my advice. Attempt to significantly reduce your social media and cell phone screen time, while understanding that complete elimination is likely not feasible. You will find an almost immediate and overwhelming positive change. Your world will instantly have a different feel. Subconscious feelings of guilt, resentment, jealousy, and hatred will occur much less often. You will free up lost time, usually hours per day. With more free time you can focus on the important relationships in your life, your career and personal growth. People will respect you and admire you in a distinct way because they will no longer have a preconceived view of who they *think* you are. They will get to know the real you—unmasked from the realm of edited pictures, exaggerated posts, and sensitive personal views.

Building a smile starts with putting down your cell phone.

Chapter 10: Be Present in the Moment

"In today's rush, we all think too much, seek too much, want too much, and forget about the joy of just being."

-Eckhart Tolle

The Magic Thread

There is an old children's story originating from France about a young boy who could never live in the present moment. This is a paraphrased version:

Once there was a boy name Peter. When he was in school, he wanted to be back home playing outside. When he was outside, he dreamed of when summer vacation would come. One day Peter fell asleep in the forest near his home. He awoke suddenly to the voice of a stunning elderly lady. She stood above him gleaming in the afternoon sunlight. As he slowly woke up, she handed him a golden ball with a small thread attached to it. She said to him, "This thread holds much power. If you pull it, time will pass much quicker. The harder you pull, the faster time will pass by."

Peter was delighted with his new gift and eager to use it. The next day, Peter was bored in math class and decided to tug slightly on the thread. Within a second, he was in the forest on a path walking home from school. A few days later he was frustrated he could not drive to the store and get ice cream, so he pulled the thread a little harder. In no time he was a teenager, driving his first car with a beautiful girlfriend in the passenger seat, on his way to the ice cream parlor.

Peter continued pulling the thread every time he became frustrated or impatient with his current place in life. If his job was not quite right, the weather wasn't what he envisioned, or his mood not perfect, he pulled the thread. Suddenly he was middle-aged man with a household of screaming kids and a nagging wife. His father had passed away, and his mother had grown frail and grey. Even he too had grey hair. Unhappy in his current position, Peter yet again looked for the thread to bail him out and change his situation.

Before long Peter found himself at the age of 92 years old. His hair was gone, and he struggled to walk. His beautiful wife had died years before. His lovely children had moved out of his house and started their own lives. As he sat there alone, he thought, for the first time in his life, about all the wonderful things he had missed out on. He had never learned to play an instrument, enjoyed the beach, planted a garden, or read a story to his children. He never enjoyed the present moment, always convinced the future would bring something better.

Distressed at this realization, Peter decided to take a walk down the same forest trail he once played on as a kid to clear his mind. He again fell asleep, and this time woke up to a voice shouting his name. "Peter!" He woke up, shocked to see the same elderly woman who had given him the golden ball with thread many years ago. "Did you enjoy my gift?" she asked him.

"I loved it at first," he said, "but I realized it was a curse. Life has passed and I never took the time to enjoy its offerings. Sure, there would have been bad times as well as great times, but I haven't had the chance to experience either. I feel empty inside. I have missed the gift of living." The old lady listened carefully and said to him, "I will grant you one more wish today." Peter said, "Let me go back to the days when I was in grade school and live my life all over again."

Peter immediately fell asleep again and was awakened this time by a different woman's voice. "Peter! You are going to be late for school!" He found himself in his childhood bedroom. To his joy and amazement, the voice calling him was his mother's. She was young and full of energy. He was again a schoolboy. He darted out of bed, eager to take on the day and start his life again. He would go on to live a full life, with many heartbreaks and accomplishments on the way. There would be laughs, smiles, regrets and tears, but Peter would embrace every one of them. He obtained the greatest gift, learning to live in the present moment.[33]

Just like Peter, we all yearn for better days. We all grow full of impatience and wish things would just move along, sometimes forgetting to let the simple things in life sink in. This story reminds us all to embrace the good and bad of each day and to recognize that being in the present moment can sometimes be the greatest gift. What a tragedy to look back at life with regret at having not lived it completely.

Live in the Now

Spiritual teacher and bestselling author Eckhart Tolle has spent a major portion of his career stressing the importance of living in the now. In many of his teachings, including his book *The Power of Now*, he explains how most people are constantly focused with the future. This, he states, is the normal state of human of consciousness.

Where will I go next? What is my next move? He explains that our ego often ignores the present moment in a desire to look to the next moment for satisfaction, creating an obsession with the future. Everyone lives as if the next moment is more important than now.

Some people, according to Tolle, seem to see the present moment as an obstacle. "Get out of the way, I need to get *there*." Others turn the NOW into an enemy. He explains, they can go into the most wonderful place, and after five minutes, they will find the one thing that's not working as it should. "They should do something about this, if not, I am going to do something about it!" they rage. If people are not complaining out loud, they are complaining in their heads about situations, about other people, that something that should be happening is not happening. Eckhart says, "This is the dysfunctional state of consciousness which is condemned to be perpetually discontent."

This concept is simple yet incredibly important. Much of human suffering and discontent stems from our obsession with the past and the future, rather than embracing the present moment. We are often in a state of constant worry about a place in time that does not exist. We dread having to go to work or take a test or pay a bill, instead of enjoying what the present moment can offer. That's not to say that paying bills and studying for tests are not important. Of course, life comes with basic requirements, and preparing for the future is surely one of them. It is when the anticipation of the future leads to worry and stress that we need to step back and readdress the rationale of diverting focus to such thoughts. When the present moment is spiraling into a constant state of discontent we need to perhaps stop thinking and be present.

Have you ever caught yourself having to do everything in your power to stop yourself from speaking when someone is asking you a question or telling you a story? One common example of our obsession with the future is the inability to listen when someone else is speaking. Instead, most people's minds are churning with countering ideas or a story to match, focusing on a response before the other person is even finished with their thought. We are so focused on a future response that we refuse to listen effectively. We do this because we subconsciously see another person speaking as an obstacle to the future satisfaction of speaking our mind.

There are entire classes and books devoted to living more in the present moment and being mindful. Utilizing some of the many resources available will help you be the best version of yourself.

Stop Worrying and Start Acting

There is perhaps no greater burden in life than worrying about someone or something. The roots of anxiety grow deep in the soil of worry about the future or something that has occurred in the past. But does worrying about the future help make it more predictable or easier to handle? Does worrying about the past make it go away? The hard-to-swallow truth is that the act of worrying does nothing but burden the present moment with fear and anxiety. It accomplishes nothing, as the past is complete, and the future does not exist.

Most people worry about things they have zero control over, instead of focusing their action on things they can control and planning appropriately for the future. *What will the weather be on my wedding day? Will I lose my job? Will I get sick from a certain disease?* We cannot control the weather, the job market, or the bad luck of illness. But we can try to stack the cards in our favor to help reduce the anxiety of unknown future events. Perhaps plan an alternate wedding venue in case the weather is not ideal, always be on the lookout for new jobs, try to save money, be healthy, exercise, eat well. Only action can extinguish the burden of worry if it has laid its eggs in your mind.

Mark Twain echoed the idea of action helping to cure worry, saying "I have spent most of my time worrying about things that have never happened. Worrying is not an action! In fact, it is action that alleviates concern and dissipates worries. Take more actions when you feel that worry is creeping in to steal your time. It need not be a huge action, any action in the direction you want to go will do."

The Importance of Reducing Anxiety

By attempting to be more present, less consumed with past and future events, we will inherently become more successful in decreasing our feelings of anxiety. No book, counseling session, or medication will ever eliminate all anxiety from our emotional make up. In fact, mild anxiety (or worrying) can be described as necessary, as it often promotes caution in times where it is necessary; this was likely developed via evolution. Appropriate anxiety is quite different than the debilitating obsession with the future or past, which can turn people into prisoners of their own minds rather than the wardens of the present. For some people, this obsession can present itself as constant worry (more of a bad habit) or as general anxiety disorder (a true mental illness). Differentiating between the two is important, as one may require medical therapy beyond a self-help book.

In addition to clouding the present moment, anxiety and worry can have major short- and long-term health effects. Thirty-five percent of people with general anxiety disorder (defined as chronic and persistent worry for over six months) self-medicate with alcohol or other drugs. They are also more prone to depression, often spiraling into insomnia, fatigue, and the inability to experience pleasure. People with this disorder are also at a higher risk of other medical conditions such as chronic pain syndromes, asthma, and inflammatory bowel disease. [34]

Seven Ways to Be More Present and Reduce Anxiety

By being more present in the moment, we will better allow ourselves to enjoy the current pleasures that life offers; decreasing our focus on the past and future, which will in turn reduce anxiety. Reducing anxiety will inherently lead to a healthier and happier you. To better live in the present moment, try these simple tips:

1. Reduce distractions. Put your cell phone down. Our constant connection with others and the perpetual state of looking down at our phones, will make it impossible to ever be present. You can take every mindfulness course on the planet, do yoga five times a day, and convince your mind *ad nauseum* to be present, but until you can gather the strength to walk away from your cell phone from time to time, all your efforts will always come up short.

2. Remind yourself. You cannot change the past and the future does not exist. Remembering this helps you realize that the only thing that truly matters is this very moment in time. Enjoy it.

3. Utilize ACTION to help reduce any worry that does exist. One of the best extinguishers of worry is tangible change, good planning and an action plan.

4. Exercise often. There is no greater natural mood stabilizer. It is a distraction from the past and future, and has countless physical and emotional benefits. Take advantage of this tool.

5. Avoid using the present moment as an obstacle to something in the future you deem more satisfying. Instead, embrace the now as a gift.

6. Take time to listen to others. It is a good exercise in patience, and more importantly, a powerful way to better live in the moment. In fact, you might learn a thing or two about the person you are listening to.

7. Meditate and learn mindfulness. The list of books, online courses, and blogs where you can learn mindfulness is endless. Take some time learning and reading about these resources.

Building a smile starts with being present.

Chapter 11: Be Patient, but Do Not Wait Around

"Two things define you: your patience when you have nothing, and your attitude when you have everything."

–George Bernard Shaw

I have struggled with perhaps nothing more in my life than learning the art of patience. For example, when I met a girl I liked, I wanted to date her now and marry her tomorrow. Of course with time, I realized that not only did I scare off a lot of good women, but my impatience also led me to be involved with some wrong women along the way. With the woman who is now my wife, I wanted to marry her by date number three. I was lucky she wanted to do the same, and even more fortunate she went on to make an amazing wife and mother. Occasionally we get lucky.

My impatience has resulted in purchasing cheaper products because I did not want to save up the money to buy something of higher quality. I am busy replacing many of those items now. I nearly abandoned my dream of being a physician because I feared failure, but also because I did not want to put in the time and sacrifice early in the process. The negative results of my inability to be patient are plentiful. I imagine it's possible to grow a garden, raise a family, advance within your career or expand your mind without patience. But with a touch of patience, your garden will reap more fruit, your family will provide more satisfaction, your career more opportunities and the potential of expanding your mind will be endless. Anything in life worth something takes a bit of sacrifice and *patience*.

A World of Instant Gratification

It is no wonder that I and most of my generation lack patience. We live in a time when we can use a cell phone to literally order any product we desire-instantly, without even speaking to another person. No packing the kids in a minivan, driving down the highway, parking and getting a shopping cart. No typing credit card numbers or going to an ATM to get cash. Just two clicks, and in three seconds the process is complete. If you do not want to click, then just tell Alexa exactly what to buy. She will handle the leg work. It's no surprise that by January 2020, consumers held over a trillion dollars in credit card debt, likely influenced by the ease of purchasing goods. [35]

Speaking of Alexa, how we listen to music and watch TV has evolved immensely. With on-demand entertainment, we have the exact song, movie, or show we want, available whenever we want. We are in full control all the time. Believe it or not, there was a period in history not long ago when we had to drive to Blockbuster to rent a movie. Imagine that! Previous generations grew up waiting. It is likely, before the advent of powerful technology, that generations before now learned patience at a much younger age. I have little doubt that they are stronger for the enhanced development of this virtue.

Recently, I have found myself ordering takeout and delivery food only from places that allow for online ordering, or making reservations at restaurants that use an online platform. Why? I do not want to take the extra two minutes to speak with someone on the phone. How pitiful. How many opportunities have I missed out on just because I do not want to give up two minutes of my time?

The examples of instant gratification are endless in today's society. College degrees can be obtained online in half the time. Major purchases can be completed before we have the money via high-interest loans. We can shop for a new home simply by swiping through an online listing. These are examples of how technology has made our lives easier and more efficient, but the price we are paying is the establishment of a generation that lacks patience.

Learning to Sacrifice

My pursuit of medicine tamed my impatience in a way I could never have predicted. Becoming a physician is a long, drawn-out process, and it is extremely easy to become impatient along the way. Think about this: from childhood, I have spent 25 years in formal education. High school, four years of undergraduate school, four years of medical school, three years of residency, and two years of fellowship. Other physicians, such as specialized surgeons, go to school for years longer than this. Patience is forced upon most who pursue medicine, and sacrifice becomes the foundation of such ambitions.

To quote financial guru and author Dave Ramsey, "Live now like no one else will, so you can live later like no one else can." These simple words carried me through many difficult times during my road through adulthood. I knew, that if

I could sacrifice in the moment, it could potentially lead to major advantages in life. This has been one of the major foundations in my approach to leadership in the workplace and decisions within my personal life.

This is not a new concept; it is an idea held by many successful individuals. Author James Allen said, "He who would accomplish little must sacrifice little; he who would achieve much must sacrifice much; he who would attain highly must sacrifice highly." This means "giving up something that is important or valued for the sake of other considerations." For example, we may have to forgo watching a TV show in order to study for an upcoming exam, not give in to sexual temptation in order to sustain a marriage and remain true to a partner, or quit a bad habit for the long-term health of our body. Whatever we give up now will pay back dividends in the future.

Of course (in reference to our last chapter) we cannot let the hope of a better future prevent us from enjoying and embracing the present moment, either. However, if we acknowledge and accept giving up something now, it can help us see the present moment even more clearly.

Choose wisely what to sacrifice now. Find ways to enjoy balancing the now with appropriately setting yourself up to be rewarded in the future. This can be challenging, but it will teach you the virtue of patience, and help you stay present and not miss opportunities when they arise.

Don't Wait Around

Like everything else in life, there is a sweet spot. Too much ambition, and you will never be content, will become self-consumed, and can neglect the feelings of others during your never-ending pursuits. Not enough ambition, and you can end up unable to secure your own food and shelter, content with not setting long term goals and bettering yourself. If you wait too long to pick a tomato, it can become infested with worms, fall off, and rot in the soil. Pick a tomato too early and it will be green, bitter, and small, having never reached its full potential.

Like learning what to sacrifice in the present moment for future gain, striking the perfect balance between being patient but not being complacent can also be challenging. By mastering this balancing act, you will reap the benefits of time and what life can offer you. The challenging component is trying to decide when waiting around becomes no longer effective and perhaps detrimental. The virtue of patience is different than a persistent state of inaction, and recognizing this difference is imperative.

Successful and happy people tend to get things done. There is no sitting on the couch, no self-pity, no fear, no endless discussions. Just action and results. They do not wait around for opportunity to knock on their door. They are ready to sacrifice and put in the hard work. This action and sacrifice will open all the doors life can offer. I cannot stress enough that waiting around for a big break in life is not practicing patience. Waiting stems from fear of failure, laziness, and blooms from a spiral of inaction. Politician and former Governor of New York Mario Cuomo said, "There are only two rules for being successful. One, figure out exactly what you want to do, and two, do it." Action.

My first "act now" epiphany occurred at the end of college when I abruptly decided to go to medical school in Mexico. The opportunity presented itself. It involved immediate sacrifice and risk, but for a long-term prize. At that time, I recognized that most college students abandoned their dreams of being a doctor because they could not get into medical school in the United Sates. In fact, as of 2017, 40% of pre-med students in undergraduate school did not go on to become doctors. [36] It is not that these students do not have the intellect. What they did perhaps lack was the willingness to take a risk and accept failure as well as the acceptance of immediate sacrifice and action.

I was not a fan of waiting around two or three more years to bring up my GPA and pad a resume, so a specific school's name could decorate my diploma. I chose to turn a decision and ambition into immediate action, and was willing to sacrifice. In the end, through failure, patience, and action, I found an amazing career. I have acted swiftly and sacrificed repeatedly since my decision to go abroad, always being patient in the process. My career in medicine has been a never-ending lesson in the importance of action.

To quote my grandmother, "You gotta bale the hay while the sun is shining." Now is your chance. Go after what you want in life and be willing to sacrifice to make your ambition a reality. Put the required time in and learn to balance present pleasure with long-term gain. Learn when to pick the tomato off the vine in life to enjoy the sweet and juicy benefits of patience and well-timed action. Do not wait around. You must search for the open doors of opportunity, and if the door is closed, knock it down.

Building a smile starts with learning patience, but never waiting around.

Chapter 12: Laugh Often. Sometimes at Yourself. Sometimes at Your Life

"Nothing is worth more than laughter. It is strength to laugh and to abandon oneself, to be light."

–Frida Kahlo

The Three Things We Should Do Every Day

Remember the kid growing up who would overreact to harmless insults? A small dig at their haircut or outfit and they spiraled into a defensive tantrum. If they got a B+ on a final exam, it was the end of the world.

These individuals were raised with poor perspective, and their hypersensitivity and misunderstanding of how seriously we should take life may have been planted early. Hopefully, a few of these kids learned as they grew into adulthood how to better handle life's rough times. Somewhere along the line, I hope that those sometimes-entitled children had an awakening, realizing that no one is getting out of here alive. I hope they learned to smile, laugh, and take part in some moderate self-deprecation from time to time.

Working hard, sacrificing, moving your way to the top and trying to be the best version of yourself is a noble undertaking. Not learning to have fun in the process and lacking the ability to make light of life when it throws us curve balls does life a disservice. Not taking the time to laugh and smile will keep you from letting go of life's iron grip of worry, tragedy, and imperfections.

What is the point of bettering yourself if you do not find happiness in the process?

Certain people you meet will bring you back down to Earth, reminding you of your mortality and what is important in life. College basketball coach Jim Valvano is one of those people. He is remembered not so much for his achievement of winning the 1983 National Championship, but more for the kind of man he was, and his passion and joy for life. In 1992, Coach Valvano was diagnosed with terminal cancer. That next year, two months before his death, he would make one of the most motivating and moving speeches in sports history at the 1993 ESPY awards. I am moved by these words every time I read or hear them.

"To me, there are three things we all should do every day. We should do them every day of our lives. Number one is laugh. You should laugh every day. Number two is think. You should spend some time in thought. And number three is you should have your emotions moved to tears, could be happiness or joy. But think about it. If you laugh, you think, and you cry, that's a full day. That's a heck of a day. You do that seven days a week, you're going to have something special." [37]

Simple, yet moving. Coach Valvano understood life. Faced with death far earlier than planned, his own mortality became a podium for hope and motivation. In his short life, he *lived* far more than any of us ever will. Take the trials and tribulations of life lightly but take his words to heart.

Learning to Laugh

There may be no greater stress in life than being an intensive-care physician on the verge of a pandemic. Despite using many of the tactics in this book, when COVID-19 hit, I would at times struggle with my emotional grasp of what the future held. As my colleagues and I watched the evolving situation from North Jersey and NYC trickle into the news networks, we were faced with the anticipation of a humanitarian crisis and an enemy we poorly understood. Just 90 miles north, they were filling up their cafeterias with overflow ICU patients. What would our hospital look like in three weeks? Fear, uncertainty, frustration, anxiety—these were just a handful of the emotions we shared during our daily COVID-19 briefings as winter turned to spring. While at that time we had not yet had a single case in our hospital or area, the tension in that room often made it feel like otherwise.

It was a cool Sunday afternoon when my cell phone rang. "It's here." I will remember those words for quite some time. "It" was COVID-19, and the first case had arrived through the emergency room. I was swarmed with fear and unease. Despite having known that the virus would eventually make its way through our doors, its arrival felt surreal.

Soon, the new cases began to pile up, and the plans we had meticulously made became a reality. During the height of the outbreak at my primary hospital site, all the active clinical sites surged beyond the capacity of our normal ICU. Thankfully, we were able to create additional space that functioned as a critical care area to care for the influx.

If you ever doubt the empathy and toughness of your fellow citizens, than take a stroll through the COVID-19 wards in some of the South Jersey hospitals where I work. And while I hope these units are not around long enough to give anyone this opportunity, I will always remember what they taught me in life. I started my week, during the peak of the pandemic, in a state of uncertainty, fear, and melancholy. Within hours of my first shift, it was clear that the veteran nurses and respiratory therapists would be the real heroes. They were heroes for the unbelievable care they consistently provided, but even more so, as the role models they became on how to handle the unwavering stress and fear of an invisible and deadly enemy.

The peak of the pandemic felt like any other day for these seasoned healthcare workers. While I could never see through their N95 masks, their smiles could be felt, and the positivity was contagious. During our daily patient rounds, which lasted considerably longer than usual, they made light of the cards we had all been dealt. They managed to make fun of themselves, our situation, and they taught me how to be a better leader and a better person. "Well at least my husband bought me a good life insurance plan," one nurse joked, as for the first time in our careers we were risking our lives to care for patients. They made jokes about their homemade haircuts, poorly home-schooled children, online shopping bills and newfound obsession with washing their hands. That morning, as the sun peeked up over the horizon beyond that small rural hospital, we all took a minute to laugh.

Fear and anxiety slowly evaporated as we continued working through the morning. My coworkers managed to remain incredibly respectful and focused, constantly upbeat, using humor and levity to keep us all grounded. They eased me in a time when I needed it most, just as they had eased so many patients before me.

It is not surprising that laughter helped ease my mind in a time of uncertainty. It has been understood that laughter has the potential to decrease hormones often associated with stress such as cortisol and epinephrine. In addition, endorphins secreted by laughter can help when people are uncomfortable or perhaps in a depressed mood.[38] Depleted levels of the neurotransmitter serotonin is one potential cause of depression and there is evidence supporting increased levels after laughter therapy.[39] Like eating well and exercise, laughing is just another weapon in the natural arsenal against "feeling down". Beyond making us feel better, this simple act can potentially improve important relationships. A study out of the University of North Carolina showed that time spent laughing among romantic partners was positively associated with relationship quality, closeness and social support. [40]

I consider myself a positive individual, and I use many of the tactics in this book to maintain this upbeat attitude. But the 2020 pandemic would forever bless me with a new and amazing tool. From the many healthcare workers I worked beside, I learned the power of laughter, a bit of self-deprecation, and the value in not taking life so seriously. There was no escaping reality. Once we all accepted this notion, we once again felt "normal."

My outlook changed after that first day in what would be a long several months of "pandemic critical care." I will always be thankful for the people I worked alongside, and I will carry with me the lessons they so effectively taught me. It was an education that no classroom, college degree, or science book could ever provide. The words of Coach Valvano and the courage and attitude of my coworkers will forever be engraved in my emotional makeup. There is little doubt that I am much better prepared for the next pandemic.

Building a smile starts with laughter, even in the most challenging times.

Chapter 13: Move

"Lack of activity destroys the good condition of every human being."

–Plato

How can we be the best version of ourselves? Education, hard work, self-reflection, and expanding your mind are some of the key components to reaching your full potential. The mind is powerful, and will open endless doors of opportunity as we optimize its function. However, one common mistake is that we often neglect to make the necessary improvements in the physical aspect of our existence—caring for and improving our body. Famous philosopher Gautama Buddha said, "To keep the body in good health is a duty .

. . otherwise we shall not be able to keep our mind strong and clear."

If anything has become evident, it is that the human body did not evolve to handle the modern western diet and the transition to an inactive state. Until recently, human evolution selected for the ideal genes to allow for physical exertion daily. We were built to gather food, run from predators, and chase down prey. We were not meant to sit on the couch for hours every night eating chips seasoned with a slew of ingredients that are difficult to pronounce. We were meant to be on the move, always prepping for our next physical journey, eating fresh fruit, vegetables, and game. We did not evolve to watch a four-hour marathon on a streaming network.

Besides all of the long-term benefits of exercise, which I will briefly touch on, physical activity releases strong hormones that almost instantly elevate a person's mood. Moderate physical activity causes a significant release of β-Endorphin, the hormone deemed responsible for a "runner's high." This hormone is created naturally by the human body, found in the nerves of our central and peripheral nervous systems. Like the drug morphine, this hormone can help reduce pain, decrease stress, and often lead to a sense of euphoria. Exercise literally and directly makes us feel good. [41]

In addition to a regular exercise routine, staying active in general is also pivotal to our wellbeing. This concept is more of a global lifestyle change that involves avoiding prolonged hours of inactivity. It is change that is best built into all facets of life. Walk around the house or yard when on your cell phone for a business call. Do not make it a habit to spend hours of time on the couch watching TV and playing video games. Push yourself to get at least 20 minutes of activity on most days. It is not so important what type of exercise you chose. Instead, find something active that you enjoy and do it as much as possible. Tap into your innate human desire. Your body is eager to get the blood flowing and it is your duty to return the favor.

Try to choose hobbies that you enjoy that will be beneficial to your health. Try watching TV while working out. Take the stairs, not the elevator. This lifestyle change involves choices you will make throughout your day that keep you active.

This can be truly challenging for people in certain professions, although other jobs will allow for more physical movement by nature. Unfortunately, the COVID-19 pandemic has forced many individuals to work from home, which has complicated this notion. As of 2010, nearly 50% of the population worked in a "low-activity" job. With this overall trend towards sedentary careers, it's important to establish regular habits to help keep your body functioning well.

Let's look at a few of the major advantages of physical activity:

1. Secretion of hormones that naturally **reduce pain and increase pleasure.**
2. Exercise regiments can be a good **distraction from anxiety.**
3. Psychological benefits are plentiful, and include **improved self-esteem, improved memory function in the elderly, and improvement in stress-related conditions.**
4. Exercise can **ameliorate the effects of age and chronic disease,** reduce blood pressure, stabilize the heart muscles, reduce

the occurrence of fatal arrhythmias, control body weight, decrease occurrence of diabetes, and lower cholesterol. [42]

In a nutshell, exercise can have a major positive impact on our physical and psychological health, all the while making us feel extremely good. It's the most powerful natural drug on the planet, and comes at no monetary cost. No book about happiness should ever leave out the need to stay active.

Building a smile starts with getting off the couch.

Chapter 14: Kill Them with Kindness

"When I was young, I admired clever people. Now that I am old, I admire kind people."

–Abraham Joshua Heschel

"Kill 'em with kindness" was perhaps the most famous of my father's many words of advice. To translate; when you are faced with extremely unkind individuals, always respond with escalating gentleness, despite the temptation to stoop low and match their callousness. This is challenging, but on most occasions will extinguish or kill their anger, as they will not have any worsening discontent to feed off of.

When you perish from this Earth, and you will, how do you want to be remembered? How will others feel when you are no longer there? Devastated? Relieved? Perhaps no one will even notice. Does it really matter? It is a guarantee that our bodies will all give out at some point, but I believe it is our reputation, our stories, the lessons we teach our kids, and how we make other people feel that has the potential to live for eternity.

Some people will spend their waking days and nights obsessed over the accumulation of material goods—a fancy car, expensive new dress, bigger house, a better job—never taking the time to make someone feel special. They will never put the time into real achievements which will live beyond their days. The cars and homes and thousand-dollar watches will all vanish, but the love you instilled in another human will last forever, engraved in their emotional DNA and passed on from generation to generation, through stories, changes in behavior, or motivation to do more good. Kindness, even when others are not so kind, is the most powerful force there is. This may be the simplest, yet most important tool to increase happiness and self-improvement. Amelia Earhart so appropriately said, "A single act of kindness throws out roots in all directions, and the roots spring up and make new trees."

It is not just others that you will influence by being kind, you will have a positive impact on yourself. In a large review of the available literature, researchers from the University of Oxford found that performing daily acts of kindness for just seven days resulted in improvements in wellbeing for the person performing the act. [43] This likely comes as no surprise; for example, we all know the feeling of giving a gift on Christmas, and the bliss associated with watching the receiver smile as they tear open the wrapping paper.

Beyond making yourself and others happy, there is now robust data showing that kindness can make you more effective. For example, being more compassionate within the field of healthcare has the potential to improve patient care, reduce provider burnout, and lower costs. This is beautifully outlined in the new book by Stephen Trzeciak and Anthony Mazzarelli, *Compassionomics: The Revolutionary Scientific Evidence That Caring Makes a Difference*. I would encourage others to learn more about this developing field.

Getting Ahead by Getting Along

Being kind goes hand in hand with learning to get along with others, and this will prove incredibly important as you advance your career and make efforts to better yourself. The overwhelming majority of the coworkers who I have seen terminated had major challenges with, to quote one of my bosses, "playing in the sandbox." Confrontation, grudges, and the inability to be kind in difficult situations will never make you happy and will never lead to success. No child wants angry, rude, and confrontational kids building sandcastles with them on the playground. Adults feel the same way.

An article in *the Harvard Business Review* that evaluated 51,836 leaders found that those who were deemed the most likable were also found to be the most effective. Of these leaders, only 27 were rated in the bottom quartile in terms of likability but in the top quartile in terms of leadership effectiveness. That is only 1 out of 2,000 people! Important attributes such as helping others learn, being cooperative, having a high level of integrity, being positive and taking part in random acts of kindness were all components of effective leaders.[44]

While moving ahead in your career or finding your passion involves more than simply being kind, it is a good way to start, and kindness will always support your success. As you show appreciation for others and build a strong reputation for respecting others, you will naturally excel at your daily tasks and find happiness in the process.

When Being Kind Is Tough

Being kind is not always easy. For example, a healthcare provider is sometimes faced with the anger, unhappiness, and irrational behavior of a patient (or their loved ones) facing a devastating health issue. I have been truly fortunate to deal with so many amazing families with incredible strength, appreciation, and kindness during some of the most challenging times. Most of the patients and families I deal with every day are extraordinary inspirations on how strong the human spirit can be.

On some rare occasions however, the story is not so inspiring. I have seen patients and families act so terribly to nurses, aides, and physicians, including myself, that I have been left speechless. One story will always remain in my memory when I reflect on how kindness will always prevail.

Many years ago, during my internal medicine residency, I had the pleasure of taking care of an incredibly challenging elderly couple. As the wife lay in bed receiving blood transfusions overnight in preparation for a procedure to stop the bleeding in her bowels, her husband sat in the corner of the room with glaring eyes. Like a lion tied down with fresh meat being thrown in its direction, he roared at anyone and everyone that walked into or near the room. The TV was too small, the lighting not right, the chair uncomfortable, the care was lousy. Everyone and everything was wrong. His love for his wife and his fear for her life brought out the worst in him.

The number of curse words was endless, and at times even creative. He was particularly nasty to one specific nurse who was providing most of the care to his wife. Despite being verbally abused for hours upon hours as she cleaned stool from the wife's backside, fed her ice chips, and made sure she received the blood products and medication she needed, this nurse never wavered in her care and compassion for both of those individuals. She remained gentle in her words and vigilant in her care. As time passed through the afternoon, the husband's rage escalated like a volcano bubbling over, until it suddenly stopped. I was working nearby, and the silence prompted me to look up. To my shock, I could see that caring nurse with her hand on the husband's neck. She looked back at me as I curiously approached her.

"Call a code," she said. Her hand was not gripping his neck to strike him, it was instead there to feel for a carotid artery pulse. She had noticed that he slumped over and became silent, so she acted quickly to address the change. We pulled him to the ground and started CPR as his wife was wheeled out of the room. After working on him for nearly 20 minutes, we gained a pulse and stabilized his vital signs. He had survived a massive heart attack on an already-weak heart. While he initially remained lethargic, within hours he slowly woke up and began to follow our commands. The nurse that he treated so badly was the first one to notice his crisis, and the first one to spring into action.

When he was eventually able to be released from the support of machines, with his wife in the ICU room next to him, this man had a different perspective on life. His sour attitude turned to sweet admiration. Despite his advanced age, he had perhaps learned another valuable lesson in life. That nurse never wavered in her affection and kindness, and in the end fear and anger lost another battle, easily defeated by a stronger force.

Always have faith that underneath peoples' shells of anger and discontent is goodness, appreciation, and love. Try to find the best in everyone, even if you are blinded by something that is troubling. This is the real potential of humanity and the most important way to a more fulfilling and happy life.

Building a smile starts with being kind. No matter what.

References

[1] Kong, Rowena. "The Role of Time Perception in Depression." *Journal of Depression and Anxiety* 08, no. 04 (2019). https://doi.org/10.35248/2167-1044.19.8.348.

[2] Siegel, Erika H., Jolie B. Wormwood, Karen S. Quigley, and Lisa Feldman Barrett. "Seeing What You Feel: Affect Drives Visual Perception of Structurally Neutral Faces." *Psychological Science* 29, no. 4 (2018): 496–503. https://doi.org/10.1177/0956797617741718.

[3] Unknown. "The Story of 2 Dogs." Be Legendary, September 27, 2019. https://belegendary.org/blog/2014/01/08/the-story-of-2-dogs/.

[4] de Hoog, N. and Verboon, P. (2020), Is the news making us unhappy? The influence of daily news exposure on emotional states. Br J Psychol, 111: 157-173. doi:10.1111/bjop.12389

[5] Unknown. "The Tale of Two Wolves - Nanticoke Indian Association." nanticokeindians, 2011. https://www.nanticokeindians.org/page/tale-of-two-wolves.

[6] Wikipedia contributors, "Helen Keller," *Wikipedia, The Free Encyclopedia,* https://en.wikipedia.org/w/index.php?title=Helen_Keller&oldid=970876002 (accessed August 5, 2020. Last modified August 2, 2020).

[7] Wikipedia contributors, "Oprah Winfrey," *Wikipedia, The Free Encyclopedia,* https://en.wikipedia.org/w/index.php?title=Oprah_Winfrey&oldid=971108639 (accessed and last modified on August 5, 2020.).

[8] Stöber, Joachim. "Self-Pity: Exploring the Links to Personality, Control Beliefs, and Anger." *Journal of Personality* 71, no. 2 (2003): 183–220. https://doi.org/10.1111/1467-6494.7102004.

[9] Watkins, Philip C., Kathrane Woodward, Tamara Stone, and Russell L. Kolts. "Gratitude And Happiness: Development Of A Measure Of Gratitude, And Relationships With Subjective Well-Being." *Social Behavior and Personality: an international journal* 31, no. 5 (2003): 431–51. https://doi.org/10.2224/sbp.2003.31.5.431.

[10] Meah, Asad, By, Asad MeahMy name is Asad Meah, and My name is Asad Meah. "34 Inspirational Quotes On Choices." AwakenTheGreatnessWithin, March 22, 2017. https://www.awakenthegreatnesswithin.com/34-inspirational-quotes-choices/.

[11] Grogan, David. "How Overcoming the Fear of Failure Helped Steve Jobs, Tim Ferriss and Bill Gates Succeed." CNBC. CNBC, August 8, 2017. https://www.cnbc.com/2017/08/07/how-overcoming-the-fear-of-failure-helped-steve-jobs-and-bill-gates.html.

[12] Wikipedia contributors, "Laugh-O-Gram Studio," *Wikipedia, The Free Encyclopedia,* https://en.wikipedia.org/w/index.php?title=Laugh-O-Gram_Studio&oldid=971172165 (accessed August 5, 2020).

[13] Conroy, David E., Jason P. Willow, and Jonathan N. Metzler. "Multidimensional Fear of Failure Measurement: The Performance Failure Appraisal Inventory." *Journal of Applied Sport Psychology* 14, no. 2 (2002): 76–90. https://doi.org/10.1080/10413200252907752.

[14] Zhang, Yanting, Siqin Dong, Wenjie Fang, Xiaohui Chai, Jiaojiao Mei, and Xiuzhen Fan. "Self-Efficacy for Self-Regulation and Fear of Failure as Mediators between Self-Esteem and Academic Procrastination among Undergraduates in Health Professions." *Advances in Health Sciences Education* 23, no. 4 (2018): 817–30. https://doi.org/10.1007/s10459-018-9832-3.

[15] *Tony Robbins: How to Get over Your Fear of Failure,* 2016.

https://www.youtube.com/watch?v=5jDBQVQi8qA.

[16] Newman, Mej "Power Laws, Pareto Distributions and Zipf's Law." *Contemporary Physics* 46, no. 5 (2005): 323–51. https://doi.org/10.1080/00107510500052444.

[17] Marshall, Perry. "The 80/20 Rule of Sales: How to Find Your Best Customers." Entrepreneur, October 9, 2013. https://www.entrepreneur.com/article/229294.

[18] Zimmerman, Jeff. "Applying the Pareto Principle (80-20 Rule) to Baseball." Beyond the Box Score. Beyond the Box Score, June 4, 2010. https://www.beyondtheboxscore.com/2010/6/4/1501048/applying-the-parento-principle-80.

[19] Rasmussen, Anne S., and Dorthe Berntsen. "The Reality of the Past versus the Ideality of the Future: Emotional Valence and Functional Differences between Past and Future Mental Time Travel." *Memory & Cognition* 41, no. 2 (2012): 187–200. https://doi.org/10.3758/s13421-012-0260-y.

[20] Quoidbach, Jordi, Alex M. Wood, and Michel Hansenne. "Back to the Future: the Effect of Daily Practice of Mental Time Travel into the Future on Happiness and Anxiety." *The Journal*

of Positive Psychology 4, no. 5 (2009): 349–55. https://doi.org/10.1080/17439760902992365.

[21] Kumar, Amit, Matthew A. Killingsworth, and Thomas Gilovich. "Waiting for Merlot." *Psychological Science* 25, no. 10 (2014): 1924–31. https://doi.org/10.1177/0956797614546556.

[22] Gilbert, David, and Junaida Abdullah. "A Study of the Impact of the Expectation of a Holiday on an Individual's Sense of Well-Being." *Journal of Vacation Marketing* 8, no. 4 (2002): 352–61. https://doi.org/10.1177/135676670200800406.

[23] Kosteas, Vasilios D. "Job Satisfaction and Promotions." *Industrial Relations: A Journal of Economy and Society* 50, no. 1 (2010): 174–94. https://doi.org/10.1111/j.1468-232x.2010.00630.x.

[24] Borchard, Therese J. "Are You Thin or Thick Skinned? Knowing Your Emotional Type." World of Psychology, July 8, 2018. https://psychcentral.com/blog/are-you-thin-or-thick-skinned-knowing-your-emotional-type/.

[25] Huebner, Rachel E. "A Culture of Sensitivity." *The Harvard Crimson*. Cambridge, MA, March 23, 2016.

[26] Tolle, Eckhart. Essay. In *The Power of Now: a Guide to Spiritual Enlightenment*, 67–68. Sydney, NSW: Hachette Australia, 2018.

[27] Worthington, Everett L., Charlotte Van Oyen Witvliet, Pietro Pietrini, and Andrea J. Miller. "Forgiveness, Health, and Well-Being: A Review of Evidence for Emotional Versus Decisional Forgiveness, Dispositional Forgivingness, and Reduced Unforgiveness." *Journal of Behavioral Medicine* 30, no. 4 (2007): 291–302. https://doi.org/10.1007/s10865-007-9105-8.

[28] Conklin, Audrey. "People Spending 3.1 Hours a Day on Smartphone Apps: Study." Fox Business. Fox Business, July 25, 2020. https://www.foxbusiness.com/technology/average-time-spent-phone-apps.

[29] Campanile, Guy. "60 Minutes- Brain Hacking." Episode. 49, no. 29, April 9, 2017.

[30] Boers, Elroy, Mohammad H. Afzali, Nicola Newton, and Patricia Conrod. "Association of Screen Time and Depression in Adolescence." *JAMA Pediatrics* 173, no. 9 (2019): 853. https://doi.org/10.1001/jamapediatrics.2019.1759.

[31] Lin, Liu Yi, Jaime E. Sidani, Ariel Shensa, Ana Radovic, Elizabeth Miller, Jason B. Colditz, Beth L. Hoffman, Leila M. Giles, and Brian A. Primack. "Association Between Social Media Use And Depression Among U.s. Young Adults." *Depression and Anxiety* 33, no. 4 (2016): 323–31. https://doi.org/10.1002/da.22466.

[32] McKinnon, John D., and Danny Dougherty. "Americans Hate Social Media but Can't Give It Up, WSJ/NBC News Poll Finds." The Wall Street Journal. Dow Jones & Company, April 5, 2019. https://www.wsj.com/articles/americans-agree-social-media-is-divisive-but-we-keep-using-it-11554456600.

[33] Bennett, William J. *The Book of Virtues: a Treasury of Great Moral Stories*. Toronto: CNIB, 2001.

[34] Stein, Murray B., and Jitender Sareen. "Generalized Anxiety Disorder." *New England Journal of Medicine* 373, no. 21 (2015): 2059–68. https://doi.org/10.1056/nejmcp1502514.

[35] Fay, Bill. "The U.S. Consumer Debt Crisis." Debt.org, November 7, 2019. https://www.debt.org/faqs/americans-in-debt/.

[36] Chen, Allen. "From Premed to Physician: Pursuing a Medical Career : Career Outlook," December 2017. https://www.bls.gov/careeroutlook/2017/article/premed.htm.

[37] Smith, Gary (May 10, 1993)."Jimmy vee hung in there". Sports Illustrated. 72

[38] Yim, Jongeun. "Therapeutic Benefits of Laughter in Mental Health: A Theoretical Review." *The Tohoku Journal of Experimental Medicine* 239,

no. 3 (2016): 243–49. https://doi.org/10.1620/tjem.239.243.

[39] Cha, Mi Youn, and Hae Sook Hong. "Effect and Path Analysis of Laughter Therapy on Serotonin, Depression and Quality of Life in Middle-Aged Women." *Journal of Korean Academy of Nursing* 45, no. 2 (2015): 221. https://doi.org/10.4040/jkan.2015.45.2.221.

[40] Kurtz, Laura E., and Sara B. Algoe. "Putting Laughter in Context: Shared Laughter as Behavioral Indicator of Relationship Well-Being." *Personal Relationships* 22, no. 4 (2015): 573–90. https://doi.org/10.1111/pere.12095.

[41] Veening, Jan G, and Henk P Barendregt. "The Effects of Beta-Endorphin: State Change Modification." *Fluids and Barriers of the CNS* 12, no. 1 (2015): 3. https://doi.org/10.1186/2045-8118-12-3.

[42] Fentem, P H. "ABC of Sports Medicine: Benefits of Exercise in Health and Disease." *Bmj* 308, no. 6939 (1994): 1291–95. https://doi.org/10.1136/bmj.308.6939.1291.

[43] Curry, Oliver Scott, Lee Rowland, Caspar J. Van Lissa, Sally Zlotowitz, John Mcalaney, and Harvey Whitehouse. "Happy to Help? A Systematic Review and Meta-Analysis of the Effects of Performing Acts of Kindness on the

Well-Being of the Actor." *University of Oxford*, 2016. https://doi.org/10.31219/osf.io/ytj5s.

[44] Zenger, Jack, and Joseph Folkman. "I'm the Boss! Why Should I Care If You Like Me?" Harvard Business Review, August 7, 2014. https://hbr.org/2013/05/im-the-boss-why-should-i-care.

Made in the USA
Monee, IL
17 May 2021